D0290558

# PRAISE FOR *FISCH TALES*

Bob Fisch became a retailer at birth. He understands that "retail is detail" and has been a sensational resource for me personally. He "listens," we "talk," and then he "challenges!" I have truly been able to benefit from our relationship in navigating the private equity world as well as an IPO and becoming a publicly traded company in 2015. Bob has "been there, done that!" He's been invaluable to my success. Bob's business and life successes enable him to help make the *Fisch Tales* book an important read for Millennials and Baby Boomers!

## MARK BUTLER
CEO, President, and Chairman of Ollie's Bargain Outlet—
One of the strongest retail growth companies in the USA

Bob Fisch has proven over the years to be a quick study in any situation, which helped lead to his tremendous success. But he truly excels in his ability to harness his tremendous energy, enthusiasm, and people skills to make everyone around him smarter and better. Bob's passion is most evident when he is mentoring younger generations, so there is no better person to write his *Fisch Tales* book, offering inspiring yet practical lessons on continuing to push forward in a career or in life at any age—"The Best is Yet to Come!"

## JOE TEKLITS
Managing Partner of ICR, Head of Retail and Consumer Group—
One of the leading strategic communications and advisory firms in the USA

*Fisch Tales* masterfully inspires and guides **Millennials** and **Baby Boomers** to embrace mutual mentoring, while learning how to capitalize on each other's unique strengths and weaknesses. Fisch built his successful career empowering and mentoring multiple generations and has a special ability to get the best out of those he surrounds himself with.

A must read for managers, corporate leaders, emerging executives, and anyone who wants to benefit from the two largest age demographics in the US.

## JEFF ERDMANN
Wealth Advisor, *Forbes* #1 Wealth Adviser in the USA 2016, 2017, 2018

# FISCHTALES

## THE MAKING OF A
# MILLENNIAL
# BABY BOOMER

# FISCHTALES
## THE MAKING OF A
# MILLENNIAL
# BABY BOOMER

I TEACH THEM BUSINESS.

THEY TEACH ME LIFE.

# BOB FISCH
### WITH BRUCE APAR

**Forbes**Books

Copyright © 2019 by Bob Fisch.

All rights reserved. No part of this book may be used or reproduced in any manner whatsoever without prior written consent of the author, except as provided by the United States of America copyright law.

Published by ForbesBooks, Charleston, South Carolina.
Member of Advantage Media Group.

ForbesBooks is a registered trademark, and the ForbesBooks colophon is a trademark of Forbes Media, LLC.

Printed in the United States of America.

10  9  8  7  6  5  4  3  2  1

ISBN: 978-1-94663-398-9
LCCN: 2019905897

Cover and layout design by George Stevens.

This publication is designed to provide accurate and authoritative information in regard to the subject matter covered. It is sold with the understanding that the publisher is not engaged in rendering legal, accounting, or other professional services. If legal advice or other expert assistance is required, the services of a competent professional person should be sought.

Advantage Media Group is proud to be a part of the Tree Neutral® program. Tree Neutral offsets the number of trees consumed in the production and printing of this book by taking proactive steps such as planting trees in direct proportion to the number of trees used to print books. To learn more about Tree Neutral, please visit **www.treeneutral.com**.

Since 1917, the Forbes mission has remained constant. Global Champions of Entrepreneurial Capitalism. ForbesBooks exists to further that aim by bringing the Stories, Passion, and Knowledge of top thought leaders to the forefront. ForbesBooks brings you The Best in Business. To be considered for publication, please visit **www.forbesbooks.com**.

*I dedicate this book to my personal and business families who believed in me in all the good and tough times and challenged me to push to achieve my accomplishments. This includes writing this book. I will continue to give back to help people of all generations to reach their potential and achieve their dreams. The sky is the limit!*

# TABLE OF CONTENTS

PIECES OF THE PUZZLE. . . . . . . . . . . . . . . . . . xi

INTRODUCTION . . . . . . . . . . . . . . . . . . . . . 1

CHAPTER ONE . . . . . . . . . . . . . . . . . . . . . 9
**DAY ONE AT A&S:**
**I PREDICTED MY FUTURE**

CHAPTER TWO . . . . . . . . . . . . . . . . . . . . . 23
**WHAT IS AN MBB?**

CHAPTER THREE . . . . . . . . . . . . . . . . . . . . 33
**THE CEO'S MOST IMPORTANT JOB**

CHAPTER FOUR. . . . . . . . . . . . . . . . . . . . . 47
**TRIBAL KNOWLEDGE**

CHAPTER FIVE . . . . . . . . . . . . . . . . . . . . . 65
**BOB'S CLUB IS NO BOYS' CLUB**

CHAPTER SIX. . . . . . . . . . . . . . . . . . . . . . 73
**THE DISRUPTOR**

CHAPTER SEVEN . . . . . . . . . . . . . . . . . . . . 83
**SHITTIN' A BRICK**

CHAPTER EIGHT . . . . . . . . . . . . . . . . . . . . . 97
**FROM LITTLE GUY TO MARKET MOVER**

CHAPTER NINE . . . . . . . . . . . . . . . . . . . . . . 111
**THE REAL DEALS: LEADERS I HAVE LEARNED FROM**

CHAPTER TEN . . . . . . . . . . . . . . . . . . . . . . 131
**DO YOU rue? I DO!**

CHAPTER ELEVEN . . . . . . . . . . . . . . . . . . . . 155
**GOING PUBLIC, GOING PRIVATE**

CHAPTER TWELVE . . . . . . . . . . . . . . . . . . . . 171
**WHAT MOTIVATES YOU?**

CHAPTER THIRTEEN . . . . . . . . . . . . . . . . . . . 179
**LISTENING**

CHAPTER FOURTEEN . . . . . . . . . . . . . . . . . . . 195
**THE BEST IS YET TO COME**

CHAPTER FIFTEEN . . . . . . . . . . . . . . . . . . . . 207
**DO YOU rue? I (STILL) DO!**

FISCH TALES FUNDAMENTALS . . . . . . . . . . . 220
**TEN INGREDIENTS OF SUCCESS**

THE PUZZLE . . . . . . . . . . . . . . . . . . . . . . . 223

MILLENNIAL ADVISORY BOARD:
WHO'S WHO . . . . . . . . . . . . . . . . . . . . . . . 225

# PIECES OF THE PUZZLE

Life is comprised of events that end up fitting together like pieces of a puzzle. Below are a number of "pieces" that helped build my career and life success.

As you read on, you'll see how the scattered pieces below fit together to shape my journey.

How do the pieces of your puzzle fit together?

# INTRODUCTION

## This is not a memoir.

Yes, it uses highlights of my long career in retailing to shed light on how you can get the most out of your work life and personal life. But it is less about *looking* back than it is about *giving* back. I'm not here to bring you my life story. I'm more interested in *your* life story.

You reach a point in life when the proverb "It is better to give than to receive" is more than mere words. It is an itch you must scratch. This book gives me a chance to do that. I'm grateful you've picked it up to find out what this *#MillennialBabyBoomer* business is all about.

When the words *Millennial* and *Baby Boomer* are used in the same sentence, rarely is it to connect the two generations in a show of solidarity.

*Fisch Tales* brings those two distinct demographic groups together to illustrate how they can learn valuable lessons from each other simply by listening more closely and sharing more freely.

Instead of gene-splicing, think *Generation Splicing*.

## WORKING ACROSS GENERATIONS

Different generations should not behave as if we're on different sides. We only benefit by interacting and learning from each other. That's why I wrote this book and why, I assume, you're reading it. It explains why I genuinely feel like I am a *Millennial Baby Boomer*. Where is it written that anyone, including me, must be tied only to one generation?

It's true that generations are categorized by a range of birth years. For *Baby Boomers*, it's 1946–1964. For *Millennials*, 1981–1996.

But beyond those bookends, everyone, no matter what age, lives in the new *Millennium*. In that respect, we all are *Millennials*, regardless of when we were born. That's how I think of myself. I don't choose my wardrobe or my cultural preferences with a conscious thought about my age. I choose them based on my personal taste. That's how I stay young! I don't let myself be pigeonholed by some generic, cookie-cutter version of how a *Baby Boomer* is supposed to look or think.

**No artificial barriers should divide the generations.**

Most of all, no artificial barriers should divide the generations. If we are to understand each other more fully, we should try to embody mutual values and best practices in how to create an ideal quality of life, how to face the future for mutual enrichment, and how to give back to each other and to society at large. I look forward to meeting and learning about other *Millennial Baby Boomers* who follow the same path I have and who feel the same as I do.

I get great enjoyment from hearing the life experiences and points of view of people who are much younger than me. Everyone's outlook is valuable to hear and understand, whether or not you agree with it. You need insight into the attitudes of people you are *Mentoring* before you can help them expand their worldview.

## WHO SHOULD READ *FISCH TALES*?

This book will resonate with anyone who identifies with one of these three groups:

- *Millennial Entrepreneurs* no doubt will recognize situations you've already encountered, or that you will come across in the course of your business education and growth. I'm confident you'll be able to find your own answers when facing situations similar to those described here.

- This book also speaks volumes to *Retail Intrapreneurs*, those who work within an established company and have the fire and ambition to rise above everyone else.

- There's value to be gained here as well for those who proudly think of themselves as *Ageless Baby Boomers*. If you're starting an exciting next phase in your life, you'll find encouragement here to proceed full speed ahead.

At the heart of *Fisch Tales* is the practice of *#MutualMentoring*. It is something I have advocated for and enjoyed my entire career, during which I have worked alongside the likes of retail legends *Mickey Drexler* (*The Gap*) and Luxottica's *Leonardo Del Vecchio* (*LensCrafters, Ray-Ban*), as well as working with *Tommy Hilfiger*.

Now, tapping into my decades of eye-opening and business-building experiences, I am able to devote even more time and energy to paying it forward, while at the same time continuing my own education in living an ageless, *Fearless* life.

It is my desire that your experience with *Fisch Tales* creates your own aha moment. My job as your *Mentor* is to get you there sooner rather than later.

The secret to making that epiphany happen is staring us right in the *ear. Listening* is arguably our most underdeveloped skill. It takes discipline and sincerity, but the rewards are well worth the effort. Simply put, you cannot grow and prosper without paying attention to what others have to say. Life is a team sport.

## PEOPLE POWER

I always instinctively put *people* and the needs of the business first. If the people around you aren't doing well, aren't happy in their work, and aren't fairly compensated, the business eventually will suffer. I don't know any way to run a business other than to take good care of the people who can make you or break you.

We all want to be fortunate in what we do. We want things to break our way. Being *fortunate*, though, is not what this book is about. That word is too passive for me, and one thing I am not is passive. I'm constantly in motion. Is the same true for you? Because the way you make yourself fortunate is by never standing still and by always working to make things happen. You must make your own fortune—and I don't mean that strictly in a monetary sense.

I didn't choose my career path or make strategic decisions based on how much money it would bring me personally. In fact, as you'll see in chapter 1, when I held my first job, I turned down a much better-paying job to stay put. It was one of the best decisions I've ever made.

Had I impulsively taken the higher-paying gig, reaching for the bigger bucks, it would have set my career on a much different path, and it's likely this book would not exist. Were it not for a *Mentor* who guided me as a father would, I might not have made what turned out to be the wise choice—the career-defining choice.

This man saw something in me of greater value than I saw in myself at the time. In a very real sense, he saved me with his inspiring words. That's how I feel about the *Millennials* I *Mentor*. I work hard to get them to believe in themselves. I admire their belief that quality of life is as much a measure of success as money. That's absolutely the right attitude.

In that first job, earning more money by jumping to the next job too soon was not a motivating factor for me. I enjoyed what I did, and that was more important. I knew that if I worked hard and pushed hard for what I believed in, it would benefit the business I was responsible for managing; it would benefit others who worked with me; and, ultimately, it would benefit me as well. It benefited me beyond my wildest expectations.

## I DON'T DO THEORIES

*Fisch Tales* will show you how to put yourself in the driver's seat of your future. I draw upon pertinent stories from my career to offer pointers that you can use in your own career. What you'll read here are not theories. I'm not interested in boring anybody with what I *think might work*. I want to help you succeed by sharing what I *know works*.

When you love what you do, work doesn't feel like labor. It becomes more possible to create amazing results and build legacies. First, you must decide what you want, how much you want it, and how to go about getting it.

Sprinkled throughout the book, interlaced with anecdotes from my varied business adventures and successes, are *School of Fisch Lessons*. They amplify real-life experiences with more generalized advice that can be put to good use in almost any profession or personal situation.

Prior to writing the book, I formed a *Millennial Advisory Board*. Its members contribute indispensable insights that account for the book's genuine empathy toward *Millennials*. Much of the misunderstanding that occurs among generations results from assumptions made at a distance, instead of information based on direct contact. Email and social media are great ways to keep in touch but, for me, nothing ever will replace face-to-face, in-person connections.

The benefits I have found from communicating openly and constructively with the younger generation are displayed on the book's cover: *I teach them business. They teach me life.* They also have touched my life. I wrote this book to do the same for others.

*Millennial Baby Boomer* is more than a book handle. It also is the nucleus of a unique mystique that speaks equally to both *Millennials* and *Baby Boomers*.

There is a great deal the generations can learn from each other. If you pick up even a couple of ideas in these pages that help you succeed, then I will have succeeded. And we both will have gained from connecting with each other.

## THE BEST IS YET TO COME

My greatest business success came after the age of fifty. For *Millennials*, the core message is this: don't be impatient, and prepare better for the future. For *Baby Boomers*, the message is this: you're just getting started on a new phase of life that can continue to be highly productive, and even more satisfying than your previous years, so do not isolate yourself from the joy of youthful pursuits.

As this book celebrates in several places, no matter your age, your attitude must be the same: *The Best Is Yet to Come!*

# CHAPTER ONE

# DAY ONE AT A&S:
# I PREDICTED MY FUTURE

**June 12, 1973.** First day on my first job. I was in the executive training program at Abraham & Straus. Based in New York City, it was considered the leading US department store chain.

If you wanted a career in retailing, A&S was like going to Harvard. It was best in class. I was determined also to be best in class. To go straight to the head of the class. What drove me? In a word, *Passion*. It has always burned in me. I can't fully explain why. It's just there.

Don't underestimate the power of *Passion*. It empowered me to take charge of my destiny. It can take you places you never dreamed of. It took me places I *did* dream of—I

Abraham & Straus, where I started my retail career.

even kept a timeline of how long it would take me to get there. I usually arrived on or close to schedule.

You need to believe you can do **Whatever It Takes** to get what you want in life. *Whatever It Takes!* That's one of my mantras in business, and in life. I don't just accept what I hear in every instance, especially when I hear "No," or "We've never done it that way." That's when I dig my heels in deep and prepare for battle.

It's about sticking to your values, following your gut instincts, and not being easily discouraged. Besides, "We've never done it that way" is BS, the kind of response you might get from people with little or no imagination.

I like to go my own way. So far, it's gotten me most of what I want out of life. I'm not talking about money here. That's a yardstick, not a goal. I'm talking about self-worth and fulfillment. Money does not buy happiness. However, happiness in your work does buy results—and that's what should earn you the money you deserve.

Making the best choices at every point in your career path is putting together the *Pieces of the Puzzle*. Don't let somebody else determine your path. Figure out what you want and what you need to build a fulfilling and productive life. Others can *feed* your passion. What they can't do is jump-start your passion. It has to burn from within.

## MENTORS MAKE A DIFFERENCE

A core step in career development is to engage someone you respect and admire to become your *Mentor*. With rare exceptions, people who have the experience and wisdom to coach you will be flattered that you asked for their guidance. Give them license to show you the way—and, at the same time, don't let anyone get in your way.

I didn't wait for a *Mentor* to show up. I went after one.

If I've learned anything from playing and studying sports, it's the importance of elevating my game, expanding my skill set, and feeding my passion.

You could say I was spoiled in getting my retail and business education at A&S. Looking back now, it was an unusually fortunate time for someone like me. I had a thirst to soak up as much knowledge as I could as fast as I could, not unlike the *Millennials* I *Mentor* today. As a twenty-something *Baby Boomer*, I had what today can be called a *Millennial* mindset: I wanted *short-term gratification*, and I was more than ready, willing, and able to put in the work required to justify my high standards.

## RETAIL ROCK STARS

At A&S, we were the beneficiaries of an all-star cast of *Mentors*. They were retail rock stars who continued to dominate the industry for years ahead.

After earning his stripes as a merchandise manager at A&S, *Mickey Drexler* transformed apparel retailing dramatically. He reinvigorated Gap, created Old Navy, and led J.Crew to new heights.

*Michael Jeffries* moved from the juniors' division at A&S to A&F, namely *Abercrombie & Fitch*. Jeffries turned a century-old, stodgy retailer into the best and hippest teen apparel merchant in

## GET A MENTOR!

One way for **Millennials**, or someone of any age, to achieve their goals is to seek the guidance of a **Mentor**. Learning the ropes from the right person is a proven way to increase your value to your employer. It's like being an apprentice. Even if you are not totally new at your job, there's always something to learn from more seasoned people willing to share their professional knowledge and street smarts. It is one of the best ways to move past colleagues who may be competing with you to land a coveted position.

If you don't make a focused effort to find a **Mentor**, the alternative is to hope that maybe someone will take you under his or her wing. Wrong! Hoping gets you nowhere fast. Maybe doesn't cut it. Waiting wastes your precious time. I never hope and wait for maybe to come along. Neither should you. Go out there and get the job done now! Success isn't built on maybes.

A&S was a magnet for the best and the brightest in the business. They belonged to the so-called **Silent Generation**, who in turn passed their smarts along to the next generation, namely the **Baby Boomers** (like me), who were moving up the ranks of companies in the 1960s–1980s.

the US. An antiquated brand was reborn as a trendy logo. There is no better business example than Abercrombie & Fitch of how a company's name is less important to its success than what it sells, and how consumers perceive that name.

## COMPANY PRESIDENT BY THIRTY-FIVE?

At A&S, the first higher-up who I encountered immediately made a life-changing impression on me. I was among 125 executive trainees sitting in orientation on that first day. We were *Listening* to the big boss, A&S CEO *Ed Goodman*.

I can't speak for the other 124 *Boomers* facing him that day, but I was fixated on every word Goodman uttered. So much so that, these many years later, I remember word for word what he told us A&S rookies: *One of you in this room in three years will be a buyer; in five years that person will be a merchandise manager; in eight years that same person will be a general merchandise manager; and after twelve years, he or she will be a president.*

Other trainees sitting around me could be forgiven if they processed that prediction as happy talk—in other words, closer to fantasy than to reality. After all, what Goodman reeled off was an intimidating timeline of aggressive goals. Our work life has barely begun, and this guy thinks one of us will make president by age thirty-five? Seriously?

I fully appreciate that, against the backdrop of today's brash, young tech upstarts, that ambitious aspiration may not sound unusual. Forty or so years ago, it was a different story. You'd be ahead of the curve to be a president at age fifty, let alone to earn that distinction in your midthirties.

As Goodman put forth his big challenge, daring each of us to meet those milestones, I realized what I wanted more than anything was to be "the one" who fulfilled that fast track to the top. What we heard may have sounded like a fantasy to the others. To me, it was an *epiphany*. "I can do that!" I thought. You can call it bragging. I call it confidence. Better yet, call it instant *obsession*.

Being *obsessed* stirs the juices, making you also *fearless, driven,* and *focused*. Having qualities like those in your toolbox is a lifelong advantage, whatever your generation—**Baby Boomer, Millennial, Gen X,** or **Gen Z.**

It doesn't take money to make the first necessary investment in your future; instead, it takes a wholehearted belief in yourself. Bring that belief to life with a plan of action, and then follow through on the action. Don't overthink the plan, or all you will accomplish is procrastination, which is the *enemy* of action. Don't slow your pace with *analysis paralysis*. Super achievers like **Steve Jobs** or **Tiger Woods** didn't *think* their way to greatness. They *obsessively* fought their way there.

## GO WHERE YOUR GUT TAKES YOU

There *is* one thing you should *not* fight: Your gut instinct. Nobody knows you better than you do. When the urge strikes, if it feels right, go with it. I did. Time and again.

Let me explain.

Up until that fateful day of June 12, 1973—when I saw my future flash before me as a predestined, twelve-year plan—a career in retailing had never been on my radar.

For the year and a half leading up to my application to the A&S executive training program, I was a graduate student at Columbia University, heading toward a degree in marriage and family counseling.

To complete my studies, I needed to earn money for tuition. Initially, that was the only reason I wanted to work at A&S. It was a matter of urgency, not of career interest. What started as a *practical need* abruptly took a sharp right turn into a *revelation*.

I have an uncanny memory that recalls tiny details from decades ago, but don't ask me how I did on my Columbia graduate finals. Once A&S happened, I never went back to check my grades. Correction: A&S didn't just *happen*. I *made* it happen. All it took was a gut instinct, stoked by the fire in my belly.

## IVY LEAGUE OF RETAILING

Some memorable moments earned me big brownie points at A&S, a place that served as a lot more than merely my first employer. A&S was like an Ivy League laboratory of learning that served me well for the rest of my career. My schooling at the store became the foundation of every business I built and ran for the ensuing five decades.

As a still-new assistant manager at A&S, I was told by my boss *Jimmy Rosenthal* to call the buyer for boys' bottoms and to curse at him if he couldn't get us more Levi's jeans to meet demand. When I objected, Jimmy's ultimatum to me was crystal clear: either do as he said or lose my job.

The buyer, fifty-seven-year-old *Harry Gilman*, told me he didn't have the goods to give us. With Jimmy glaring at me as he monitored the phone call, my survival instinct kicked in.

Bracing myself for the reaction, I gritted my teeth and nervously told the man on the other end of the line, a respected thirty-plus-year veteran of A&S, to go "F" himself!

Predictably, Harry went ballistic. After Jimmy left my office, laughing, I confided to Harry that I was instructed to use the "F" bomb under duress. He still wasn't happy, but said he understood.

PS: I got the jeans we needed.

Six months later, I was made manager of the boys' department at another A&S location. One of the key supporters who helped me win that position was none other than Harry Gilman. Just goes to show that you never know when a well-placed, well-meaning curse can give a little boost to your career.

I say that with tongue in cheek, of course. The real moral of that story is: sometimes you have to play the game to show your superiors you're not afraid to **Put It on the Line**. That's a major theme that we'll revisit throughout the book.

## NO BUDGET? NO PROBLEM!

I had a similar experience when a different A&S buyer, **Alan Eisenberg**, told me he didn't have the budget to order more boys' pajamas for my department. No problem! I went around the buyer to call the vendor myself to place the order. No manager would dare do that. Except obsessive, **Fearless** me. When the shipment of jammies arrived, I unloaded and ticketed the cartons myself, guaranteeing that they would be on sale within a matter of hours, instead of the next day. The supply sold out in a few days.

When I was leaving A&S, Alan told me, "By the way, Fisch, I always knew whenever you placed orders yourself, because the vendor always called me." Yet, even then, he didn't have a problem with my unorthodox methods—because I got the job done, and my sales numbers exceeded expectations. Once again, I had **Put It on the Line**, and it paid off not only in the short run with increased sales, but also with my earning the long-term respect of those I worked with and worked for. Do you play it safe or take risks to see where they will get you?

I constantly hammer away at **Putting It on the Line** with **Millennials**. Even very successful people I **Mentor** have confided in me their insecurity about something as ordinary as being summoned to the boss's office. Panic strikes. *Am I going to be fired?!* That's not a wholly *unnatural* thought to have, but you can't let it undermine your confidence either. *Do not talk yourself into losing respect for your own abilities.*

## Do you play it safe or take risks to see where they will get you?

I have an actor friend who has been coached to walk into an audition like he owns the room. It's no different when you are performing in the theater of business. It's understandable to feel some butterflies inside when the boss calls you to an unscheduled meeting. Just don't show that you're the least bit nervous. Walk in like you're ready to explain or defend any action you've taken. Show calm and confidence in answering any question thrown at you. I'm not advising you to fake it. I'm advising you to be a model Boy Scout and always be prepared. That may mean moving outside your *comfort zone.*

## THIS IS A NO-COMFORT ZONE

Staying within your *comfort zone* can be defined, in one way, as confining yourself to the scope of your strongest skills. It also means you're not challenging yourself to become proficient in other areas that will make you more versatile and help you get ahead.

A *comfort zone* also can be your job description. Colleagues or superiors may not look kindly on those who go above and beyond their job description. Why? Because it threatens *their* comfort zone. That philosophy is more commonly known as *staying in your lane*.

That's just about the *worst* business advice I've heard: *stay in your lane*. Your *lane* is whatever path gets you to the destination you've staked out for yourself. If I always had stayed in my lane, odds are I wouldn't have built the largest specialty-apparel retailer in store count at rue21 … I wouldn't have helped several managers there become millionaires from our high-flying stock performance … and I wouldn't be writing this book. *Stay in your lane* is the fast lane to going nowhere special.

I'm not about to claim that every move I made was the best one. But missteps serve a purpose. Rebounding from your mistakes is self-education. It's a good way to develop fortitude in the face of adverse circumstances. I had my share of miscalculations during those early days at A&S. They were necessary reminders of how much I had to learn, about life as well as about business etiquette.

## SWEAT SUIT WITH CLODHOPPERS

At the end of that first day of orientation, I literally sweated out the ride home from work.

It was an unbearable ninety-eight degrees. For some crazy reason, I wore a worsted-wool Pierre Cardin suit, punctuated by a ridiculous bow tie. In my head, I had grown up overnight from college frat boy to working man. I was going to look the part. Did I mention my tri-color, high-heeled shoes, which were a bold fashion statement as the '60s turned into the '70s?

# JOB CRAFTING, ANYONE?

Process is always critical, but that doesn't mean that every process is sacred. "Well, we always have done it this way" is not a strategy for success; it's an excuse for not bothering to find a better way in the name of progress. Adam Grant, a renowned organizational psychologist who teaches at the Wharton School of Business, advocates "job crafting."

That's where you can reshape your job to play to your strengths and for the sake of efficiency. If you can improve or correct a process—even momentarily, as I did by placing orders myself to get instant results—don't just think about it. Make it happen!

Sometimes it's better to ask for forgiveness than to ask for permission.

After work, I hopped into my non-air-conditioned 1970 Chevrolet Malibu to make the trip from the Brooklyn headquarters of A&S to my new, shared apartment in the Kew Gardens, Queens, neighborhood of New York City.

It was a new route for me, and the huge steel footings of the elevated subway that I had to navigate around made it harder to be certain where I was going. This was way before GPS. By now, I'm sweating buckets—my new worsted suit, water-logged pleats and all, resembles an accordion—and I'm wondering, to quote a hit song of the day, "What Kind of Fool Am I?"

By the time I found my way home, the Cardin had become a literal sweat suit that I had to frantically peel off before I even was in the door of my apartment.

Those high-stepping shoes didn't last long, but to this day, I still have the Cardin jacket. Call me sentimental (you'd be right), but I had an inkling that the jacket would carry special *Meaning* for me later in life, and I was right: it remains a precious memento of my mostly humble beginnings.

Artist's rendering of my Cardin jacket.

As for the shoes, they almost got me off on the wrong foot, fashion-wise, but I was saved from further embarrassment by my group manager, Jimmy Rosenthal. When I showed up as his assistant manager, I was wearing those garish clodhoppers. He was so horrified, he told me to take them off right there in the store. Then Jimmy sent me in my socks to the shoe department to buy a new pair, something more befitting my junior-executive status.

Jimmy also advised me to buy a new suit every week. That was a bit much to expect on my salary, but he had made his point: dress for success, Fisch, or cut bait!

## ONE OUT OF 125

It's hard to fully explain all these years later what came over me on June 12, 1973, as I listened to Ed Goodman's milestones for that one person in 125 who wanted it badly enough to rise to the occasion again, and again, and again.

As it turned out, Goodman knew what he was talking about that day. He didn't know it at the time, but he was talking directly to me. I went on to attain each of those positions, and did it within the approximate time frame he had outlined.

Three years later, in 1976, I was promoted to buyer at A&S.

In 1978, I was named merchandise manager at Jordan Marsh in Florida.

In 1982, I became general merchandise manager at Jordan Marsh.

In 1986, I was president of the TH Mandy division of US Shoe Corporation.

One of the indirect ways that Goodman *Mentored* me occurred on his last day before retirement. This veteran executive, who was responsible for thousands of people on the A&S payroll, made the rounds to say farewell to all the managers.

As was the case with the inspiring words I heard him say on my first day, that gesture spoke to me loudly and clearly. What a classy move, I thought, for the head of the company to shake everyone's hand, mine included, and to wish us well. It stayed with me.

At *rue21*, I had the corner office, as CEOs usually do, but I managed the company by walking around, every day, to talk with as many people as I could. It's actually a recommended practice that's known, simply enough, as *management by walking around*.

Let's do that right now. Wander with me as we visit some of my other adventures in *The Making of a Millennial Baby Boomer*.

# CHAPTER TWO

# WHAT IS AN MBB?

**The year is 1970.** After discovering data that shows 76 million babies were born in the US between 1946 and 1964, a researcher gives the number a name: *Baby Boom*.

Next thing you know, *kaboom*! A nickname for a whole generation is born: ***Baby Boomers***.

Here's the thing, though: Like a caricature of someone's face, nicknames distort actual features in the name of fun.

*Baby Boomer. Millennial. Gen X. Gen Y. iGen.* Those labels describe *what* you are, not *who* you are—or, more important, who you can become! It doesn't matter what year you were born. It doesn't matter what generation you belong to. What matters is how we get along, so we can stay strong, and move along.

That's one reason I like the label ***Millennial Baby Boomer (MBB)***. It ignores any so-called "generation gap." It ignores age, which is just a number. I know I'm not the first to say that, but I'm not aware of anyone else who has created a brand like *Millennial Baby Boomer*.

That 1970 researcher named a number (76 million) the *Baby Boom*. By contrast, *Millennial Baby Boomer* captures the idea of staying ageless, at any age. In other words, *MBB* designates the *absence* of a number.

The *MBB* handle is meant to erase the barriers we put up because of age. For me, *MBB* frees the mind and the will to discover new possibilities, no matter your stage of life. I adapt with the changing times. An *MBB* is a bit of a chameleon, someone with a survival instinct.

Each of us is a one-of-a-kind creation who never stops being a work in progress. If you're not always moving forward, you stop growing. Living in the moment, while also creating a *Vision* for the future, is how your life will gather *Meaning* and *Momentum*.

My own progression, as a young man, led to the *Vision* that I could not let life just happen to me. I feared that would lead to failure. The truth is that I couldn't afford to fail. I know, and agree with, the business adage about having to fail to succeed. That's not what I mean.

I am saying that I couldn't afford to fail at *life*. I didn't have a backup plan, like a cushy inheritance. There was no family business for me to take over. I had to make it on my own.

I'm not afraid to admit that I was anxious. That's normal. I decided that the best way for me to deal with fear of failure—and to avoid failure—was to act *Fearless*.

## TAKING DOWN BARRIERS

That epiphany opened up a world of possibilities for me. I couldn't think of myself strictly as a *Baby Boomer*. That's too limiting. It's putting up barriers. I go straight through barriers. I take down barriers that get in my way or that might slow my progress. That's what I want you to do too. If you're going to fail—and you will at some point, because we all do, and it's how we learn to succeed—don't fail because of someone else's negativity. Fail on your own terms! Then learn from that failure and keep moving ahead, more determined than before. That's exactly how I operate, and it's worked out well for me, as you'll find out in this book.

When we casually generalize about a diverse crosssection of unique individuals—whether *Millennials* or *Baby Boomers*—we reduce real people to faceless statistics.

I reject that. My ability to get what I want and to further my goals is based on treating each person as someone of distinct value, a value that can be enhanced.

Values also can be shared. That is part of what being a *Millennial Baby Boomer* is about: shared values that can, and should, connect generations more closely, and more productively. If separate generations can learn to empathize more openly with other generations, their shared values have a chance to benefit everybody. Think of it as an equation: 1 + 1 = 3.

**If separate generations can learn to empathize more openly with other generations, their shared values have a chance to benefit everybody.**

*Millennials*, for example, place a high value on *Giving Back*. As *Baby Boomers* transition into their next phase of life, what better way to find fulfillment, and to invest in the generation(s) taking over the world, than by sharing decades of experience, expertise, and values with other generations? Writing this book is one of my ways of *Giving Back*—sharing my knowledge, and what I have learned from others, with the next generation of leaders.

There's a lot to admire about *Millennials*. I enjoy *Listening* to them, learning from them, and helping them in any way I can. It's *Mutual Mentoring*, which is a major theme of the book.

I admire *Millennials'* embrace of diversity, in everything from gender equality in the workforce to multicultural socialization.

*Millennials* are idealists. So am I. They are more likely to be independent in their politics than to conform their views to a rigid political label. That's me as well. They place great value on work-life balance, and why not? It's logical that people more content in their personal lives will be better workers, and of more value to coworkers and to employers.

If there's one way in which I most admire *Millennial* values— and in which I fully embody being a *Millennial Baby Boomer*— it's their courage to *Challenge the Status Quo*. That neatly sums up not only my whole career, but also explains the reason for my successes. I exercised my individual freedom. I relished the role of rebel, maverick, disruptor—whatever you want to call it.

How did I become fiercely determined, fully confident, and ultracompetitive? How does this help you? I hope it helps you achieve your dreams and understand becoming an *MBB* yourself.

As far back as I can remember, I always felt comfortable talking with—and staying in constant touch with—people outside my age group. When I was younger, I got along easily with older people. As I became older, that same affinity for reaching beyond my peer group to make comfortable connections enhanced how I worked with and related to younger people.

I always related well to people up and down the line from my age group. I wasn't judgmental in either direction. My mind works best when it stays open to all possibilities. To my way of thinking, older is not always wiser, and younger is not always inexperienced.

## NO EXPIRATION DATE ON ENTHUSIASM

There's no minimum or maximum age for embracing a zest for life. That's what gets me up in the morning, gets me to the gym, and keeps me going all day long—looking for new things to do, new people to meet, and new tasks to tackle.

Around 1981, something happened that would define my mission in life: the first *Millennials* were born. When their lives started, my life changed. For the better.

What the *Millennial* generation has going for it is not exclusive to this age bracket (born 1981–1996). They are at the time of their lives when dreams are built, and they should be having the time of their lives. Still, mistakes are made. Lifelong lessons are learned. But I tell them that *The Best Is Yet to Come*. I don't say that to make them feel good. I say it because I believe it. And I believe it because I have lived it.

After *Baby Boomers*, the 73 million *Millennials* represent the second largest generation of voters. Their influence only will become stronger, so it's in our best interests to help them and work with them, not against them.

Being a *Millennial Baby Boomer* also means recognizing that *Millennial* is more than the name of a generation. To the degree that the word describes our evolving culture, we live not only in the age of *Millennials*, but in the *Millennial Age*. They are behind evolutions in technology, transportation, work-life balance, travel, religion, politics, you name it. Dramatic shifts in social behavior and attitudes that are transforming how society functions can be attributed to the *Millennial* zeitgeist. It's almost as if there are two choices: become a forward-thinking *Millennial Baby Boomer* to assimilate better into modern times, or be content as a backward-looking twentieth-century *Baby Boomer*, waving at the shiny new world passing you by.

I'll leave it to others to dwell on the past. When I had just passed the half-century mark in age, I had been a chief executive for more than twenty years, and there was so much more I hungered to accomplish. I believed I just was getting started. My ambition was no less fierce than that of a hard-charging *Millennial* half my age.

Getting things done is my lifeblood. It's always been that way. As my career gained traction, to do my job to the best of my ability, I determined I needed to tap into the mindset of the *Millennial*.

Rather than managing down, I managed *across* the organization.

## MUTUAL R-E-S-P-E-C-T

*Mutual Mentoring* is my magic potion. How does that work? First establish a rapport with the other person, then connect on a gut level, and finally build a foundation of mutual respect.

When *Baby Boomers* were coming of age, the most popular periodical was a weekly magazine titled, simply, *Life*. In June 1968, one of its covers showed the face of a twenty-one-year-old man accompanied by two words: *Generation Gap*. The article inside was about a book called *The Gap*. After spending a summer together, the young man and his fortyish uncle wrote about their respective views on various topics as seen through the eyes of a *Baby Boomer* (the twenty-one-year-old) and a member of the so-called *Silent Generation* (born between the two World Wars). That's an early example of *Mutual Mentoring*.

## TIPS ON HOW TO BE AN MBB

The guidelines presented here are a combination of my experience and insights provided by our Millennial Advisory Board.

**Do:**

- Give Back (or Pay It Forward)
- Get to Know People for Who They Are, Not What They Are
- Keep an Open Mind to New Possibilities
- Mentor and Be Mentored
- Value Consensus
- Listen More
- Push Others to Be What They Want to Be
- Find Purpose in Your Work
- Measure "Wealth" by Your Quality of Life and Your Experience
- Solicit Feedback Continually
- Make People Feel Valuable

**Don't:**

- Prejudge People by Age or Other Labels
- Talk Down to Anyone
- Stop Striving to Learn New Skills
- Let Others Define Who You Are or What You Are Capable of Doing
- Mistake Your Priorities for Others' Priorities
- Define Wealth by Your Income or Savings
- Undermine the Enthusiasm of Others

As a *Millennial Baby Boomer*, my mission has been to bridge whatever gap may exist between these two generations, which in turn are separated by *Generation X* (born 1965–1980). You've heard of gene splicing. Think of what I do as *Generation Splicing*.

# GENERATION SPLICING

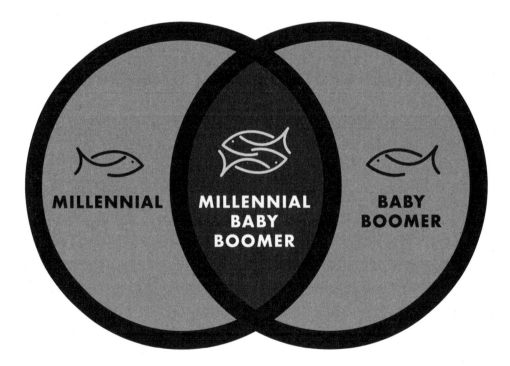

MILLENNIAL    MILLENNIAL BABY BOOMER    BABY BOOMER

Even though I am the first to use the *Generation Splicing* label of *Millennial Baby Boomer*, it doesn't mean other *Baby Boomers* can't follow the same path. All you need to do is start to listen a little more. Be more curious. Don't give in to stereotypes. Most of all, engage in *Mutual Mentoring*.

## NO COOKIE-CUTTER SOLUTION

There is no greater pleasure for me than witnessing a young person improve their quality of life, both in their work and in their other pursuits outside of work. There is no cookie-cutter blueprint that prepares you for every challenge that comes your way. Every situation calls for its own solution.

Over the years, my aptitude for learning from and helping *Millennials* has flourished. Throughout my professional life, there has been one constant: get to the next level and have fun doing it. That's a state of mind that, for me at least, never gets old.

No matter which position I have held, or what size business I have run—from a department in a single store to 1,200 stores employing twenty thousand people—my goal has never changed: get the most out of myself and out of others to set new benchmarks for personal fulfillment.

What's my job as a *Millennial Baby Boomer*?

*I teach them business.*

*They teach me life.*

# CHAPTER THREE

# THE CEO'S MOST IMPORTANT JOB

## A CEO's most important job is motivating

**people.** No matter how big you get, if you don't make associates feel integral to the success of your company, you will not get to the level you want.

My people-centered approach at rue21 took many forms.

At rue21, we had a beloved district manager from Iowa, *Jen Kane*, who bravely battled cancer for more than five years before succumbing to the disease. I can't imagine what it's like to face that kind of fear, but Jen's amazingly positive attitude and courage inspired all of us.

During her ordeal, Jen would send me upbeat notes about how eager she was to get back to work. She kept her mind off her grim situation by focusing instead on all the things she liked at work.

Mostly, she missed her coworkers. And they missed her.

After Jen passed, I told the district managers that we would dedicate rue21's back-to-school season to her. One of the morale boosters I had brought to rue21 from my prior position at Casual Corner was an award called *Whatever It Takes*.

That name says it all. *Whatever It Takes* recognition was reserved for a person who went above and beyond expectations to achieve something extraordinary that made a measurable difference in our business. We presented Jen posthumously with the *Whatever It Takes* award.

For obvious reasons, that presentation was filled with raw emotion felt by everyone in the room. People are moved to rally around an indomitable spirit, even to the extent that the poignant moment stays with them as a source of motivation well into the future.

The *Whatever It Takes* award was held in high regard within the ranks at rue21, with great admiration and respect for the recipient. The award, an elegant glass paperweight, held special *Meaning* to me. It reflected my managerial emphasis on nurturing people. That was my mantra throughout a forty-plus-year career that I continue to preach today.

Celebrating achievements should be standard practice in any business. It stirs the competitive juices, spurring others to perform at a higher level. Anyone who doesn't view the recognition of other people or other departments as an incentive to strive harder is not likely to have a bright future in the company.

Just as process needs a strategy, it also must have behind it the driving force of entrepreneurship.

No matter how hardworking or talented people may be, everyone needs encouragement and motivation. People thrive on information. They want to know what's going on behind the scenes

## COULD YOU CARE LESS ...
## OR MORE?

Caring deeply about people is a desirable core value, but caring is only half of it. The other half is not hiding it. Show them that you care. It's therapeutic.

For those not in a leadership role, show your boss(es) that you care about more than your paycheck. Demonstrate clearly that you have a personal stake in the performance of the whole company by asking questions, offering to help with tasks not in your job description, or volunteering to help a coworker. The simple act of offering assistance sets you apart from your peers.

I loved praising people who deserved it. By making everybody believe they are critical to the company's success, a manager helps others reach their goals.

Some believe **Millennials** are especially sensitive to being recognized for their efforts. But that's a legitimate expectation by people of all ages. It's a way to acknowledge someone is engaged in the job.

It's never a bad idea to show people working for you some love. That doesn't always involve a monetary reward or a title change. An achievement award goes a long way too. Meeting associates halfway in recognizing a job well done is a worthwhile way to encourage their positive attitude and amp up their output at the same time.

within their own company. Keeping them informed will encourage a sense of ownership, motivating them to do not merely a *good* job, but a *great* job.

As anyone who has worked for me can attest, doing a good job is to be expected, but that doesn't mean good is good enough. If a person wasn't good to begin with, I wouldn't have hired him or her. Good is a starting point, not the finish line.

## FROM THE DESK OF THE CEO

Each week at rue21, I sent a company newsletter called *Biz Sunday* to key managers. We employed in excess of twenty thousand people. A company that size normally has specialists who manage internal communications. Not us.

I saw the newsletter as a great way to reach across the company in my own one-to-one, informal style. I'm not a corporate speak guy. Reading important information about the company that comes directly from the CEO in plain and passionate language adds credibility and immediacy to the message.

Adding my down-to-earth commentary to the facts and figures I was sharing through the newsletter gave the numbers more relevance and made them more understandable in the framework of our business.

I wanted everyone in the company to know the nitty-gritty, not only as it affected their own business, but also to give them insight into what was happening in other parts of the company. Instead of being on the outside looking in, it placed them on the inside of everything that was going on.

*Biz Sunday* was one of many ways I made it my business to connect with the people in our company.

SCHOOL OF FISCH LESSON

## SPEAK PLAINLY AND DIRECTLY

No matter who you are communicating with, whether it's a subordinate or a boss, speak plainly and directly. In addition to sending the weekly *Biz Sunday* newsletter, I liked to walk around the support center every day to interact with as many people as I could.

My goal always was to keep the lines of communication open. You can't give direction once, walk away, and think your expectations magically will be met to your full satisfaction.

It requires repeated back and forth, constantly digging deeper to work it out. You set goals, delegate authority to achieve them, and monitor progress. That's the key to success in business.

Proof of value, profitability, and market share are achieved through the people who pick the merchandise and analyze the data. The merchandise is the fuel, but the people are the engine that has to be revved up constantly.

## INSPIRING THE TROOPS

When addressing our one hundred-plus district managers at group meetings, I would speak off the cuff for up to an hour. I told stories about how people make a difference. At the end of the meeting, I tried always to close with a story of human interest. A typical role model I used is basketball superstar *LeBron James*.

Both on and off the court, no matter which team he has played on, his bold leadership makes those around him better. Beyond his unequaled athletic gifts, King James, as he is known, has an obvious talent for motivating others to raise their game.

You'd be surprised how deep a personal connection people will make just by hearing about a success. It all comes back to the power of human-interest stories. That's why I made a habit of ending meetings with that kind of story. Invariably, there was not a dry eye in the house. That goes for me too. It was hard for me *not* to get a bit teary eyed when the group rose to applaud as the meeting ended.

## THINK FAST, ACT FASTER

One of my favorite stories took place on the night before Black Friday. It was the start of the retail trend for big-box stores to open their doors at midnight on Thanksgiving to get a jump on holiday sales activity. A quick-thinking store manager for a rue21 in South Carolina noticed a line of cars stretching from the parking lot into the street, waiting for the Walmart to open.

He immediately called the assistant store manager to say this was an excellent opportunity to also open our store, even though it was not scheduled to operate during those hours. They agreed. As a result of that action, that dynamic duo raked in $10,000 between midnight and six in the morning. Based on rue21's average transaction of $25, that was the equivalent of a sale a minute.

The ambitious manager who made an instant decision to open his store at midnight was invited to tell the story at one of the district managers' meetings. It wasn't long before he attended every meeting: we promoted him to district manager.

A field manager in any company getting a call from the CEO is not exactly commonplace. In my mind, though, even that rare occurrence isn't sufficient recognition. When I heard success stories like the spur-of-the-moment midnight store opening, I could have just picked up the phone to thank the manager and be off the call in ninety seconds. Instead, I decided, why not make the most of such great enterprise?

I saw more to be gained by putting the associate in front of everyone to showcase a shining example of how to go the extra mile.

As a CEO, I never saw my role as hovering over everyone. I dove right in to immerse myself in their day-to-day culture. I see no point in staying distant from the people you rely on every day to push your business to the limits of its potential. You can accomplish a lot of amazing things when you exercise your authority in a responsible, personal way, and try to do what you think is right.

## LEARNING ON THE JOB

I did not always play the game of high-stakes business well in the beginning. It's not that I wasn't smart. It's that I was arrogant. That doesn't go over well when you're climbing the corporate ladder. There is a very fine line between confidence and arrogance. I crossed the line early on. Instead of letting it throw me off my game, I used it to understand the meaning of humility.

I was too focused on the sound of a title. I was impatient, just like a *Millennial*. Impatience is not always a bad thing. Remember, though, that your employer is even more impatient to see what you can do. So, don't get too hung up on titles, like I did at one point.

The more a boss likes what he or she hears, the more that boss will let you do what you want. Your attitude with the boss should be, "I'm here to help you." Show them what you can do, and the rest will come. If it doesn't, make it happen somewhere else. Don't get discouraged too easily.

*Millennials* need to confront issues, especially when they would rather avoid them. It's important to confront them the right way—constructively. To help others succeed in their jobs, I learned to tell people what they need to hear and what they need to do. It's about transparency, in both directions—from manager to associate and from associate to manager.

There are other lessons from my past that have shaped my *Mentorship* of *Millennials* and my managing up as well.

## CHOOSE YOUR BATTLES WISELY

My father, *Ray Fisch*, was very talented in many ways. He also was set in his ways, and that could get him in trouble with clients or bosses. You may not agree with the other person you're dealing with, but, as I said, you have to learn to play the game of compromise. Choose your battles wisely. Not everything has to go your way.

**You learn by seeing what doesn't work.**

In learning how to work productively with people, I did the *opposite* of what my father did, so in a sense, he helped me grow and prosper. You also learn by seeing what doesn't work. Later in life, I told him what I learned from him.

I was confident enough to figure out how to deal with people to get what I want, while also making sure they felt the same satisfaction on their end. However, if you asked me twenty years ago if I knew I could create a billion-dollar business, as I did at rue21, I'd have looked at you funny. I had no idea I could do something of that magnitude when my father could not.

Like my dad, I was set in my ways. It showed itself when I worked at a company, *Jon Steed*, as a buyer. *Bob Lowenstein*, whom I had reported to previously at A&S, was once again my boss. One Friday, he told me that he wanted to start accompanying me on visits I made to vendor showrooms. Rather than comply by saying, "Sure!" I had to make my life interesting by asking him, "Why?"

Some bosses understandably would not appreciate being questioned in that way. Bob seemed hardly fazed by my response. He calmly told me that if I didn't want to adjust to accommodate him, maybe it wasn't the right job for me. He didn't have to yell or throw a fit. I got the message. I gave him my meeting schedule right away—and guess what? Bob never once came with me to an appointment.

## CREATING A BUSINESS PERSONA

I realized then that you can win simply by staying open to other points of view. It may mean moving out of your comfort zone. That's a good thing, because that is how you stretch and grow in job maturity and versatility. There are times when defending your position at all costs comes across as being defensive and insecure. It's not the kind of look you want to show the boss—or anyone, for that matter.

I worked with someone at *Jordan Marsh* who was demographically my opposite, *Tom Unrine*. I'm a brash native New Yorker. Tom was born in Green Bay, Wisconsin, and lived in Cincinnati, Ohio. His upbringing was white bread, milk, mayo, and bologna. Mine was chopped liver on an onion roll with Dr. Brown's cream soda, sour pickle on the side. You get the picture.

Tom and I would go to a store where we both felt the same ambivalence in our gut toward whomever we were seeing, yet our attitudes were starkly different: Tom would put on a smiley face. Instead of hiding my frustration, I wore it on my face. Tom subtly made people realize that they might not be right. I used blunt force, like a bulldozer, while he wielded a velvet hammer.

Bringing to bear his *Pedigree* of appearing trustworthy and welcoming as soon as he walked in the room, Tom took me aside and made no bones in telling me, "You're from New York City, so you're not going to be trusted as much. You need to be less arrogant and act more like me to get ahead."

I wasn't insulted by what he said. I always am looking to improve, so my eyes were opened. I decided that sometimes it would be wiser to wear a poker face, or to smile, no matter what I thought. Tom helped me develop a business persona. To this day, we are very good friends.

## ON THE JOB 24/7

I've had the good fortune to work with Tom and other key executives who have helped shape my outlook and career arc. Some have been at my side for decades, accompanying me from one company to the next.

Their loyalty is invaluable to me. Their loyalty also is not blind. If they disagree with me, I want to hear it. No CEO has all the answers. Any CEOs who think they do are not going to hold on for long to the brain trust they need to succeed.

I want people around me who don't watch the clock. People who get the job done no matter what time of day or day of the week it is.

That unyielding work ethic applies not just to people who report to me. When you've attained a certain position in the business world, no matter where you are, or what time it is, if somebody needs to talk to you, or vice versa, everything and anything else you are doing takes a back seat.

Maybe you are on vacation. Or on the seventeenth hole of a high-stakes golf game. You're enjoying your first cup of coffee Sunday at seven in the morning. It's ten on a Friday night and you're at a rockin' party. Doesn't matter where you are or what you're doing. You have to be available to the outside world 24/7. No excuses. Those who do make excuses for not being available don't have what it takes to lead others. Period.

## TO PROSPER, PROCESS NEEDS MOTIVATED PEOPLE

In the day-to-day competition for market share, and the struggle to "make your numbers," the difference between winners and losers is not brand or merchandise or marketing. The difference is the people who make all of that happen.

It would be easy to assume that once a tightly wound process is in place, it will take care of itself, like a well-oiled machine. It also would be wrong to assume that. Designing an efficient, profit-conscious process is critical, of course. But any process is only as effective as the people who manage it and always seek ways to improve it.

One of the things I've learned from my many experiences with *Millennials* is the advantage of *Tribal Knowledge*.

People provide the pulse and lifeblood of a company and help it get ahead. They also stay in touch with the pulse of the market. They are loyal to the company's pursuit of goals and excellence. *Tribal Knowledge* means people willing–when necessary—to sacrifice their own inclinations to achieve a common goal.

Engaging people within your organization must be a top priority. It's one of my favorite parts of being a team leader. The person at the top needs to set a tone and to empower people to fulfill the corporate mission.

Everybody has their own technique, but I always liked a little more flair.

Not every CEO is comfortable getting down with people at all levels of the company. I look forward to being in the mix, getting people to wave the company flag. That's why I am an advocate, as already stated, of *management by walking around.*

Just as I remembered the senior executives doing at A&S long ago, I also walked around the office as much as possible to say hello and talk with as many people as I had time for. I knew that if one of the A&S execs confronted me, it's because they cared about what I was doing and how I was doing. I felt the same about people working for me.

I like finding ways to engage people in fun and relatable ways. It creates a social atmosphere that helps productivity and morale. Slogans are a great way to get people in the spirit, and to get them excited about where they work. Part of it is the sports-inspired cheerleader in me. When I get excited, I want everyone to be excited. When everyone joins in on a "cheer" or a motto, it brings out the *Millennial* in me.

It's common for large organizations to show appreciation for outstanding work through awards. They might mention the awards in a company newsletter or email.

At rue21, we made a very big deal of our awards to maximize the recognition and gratitude that people received throughout the company.

We held a gala dinner-dance every March called the *ruebe* (pronounced "ruby") *Awards*. They shone a spotlight on associates and managers who were best in class in each of about twenty categories: store of the year, best sales performance, and so on.

Separately from the ruebes, once or twice a year, we presented that *Whatever It Takes* award mentioned earlier. The fact we presented the award to one person once or twice a year lent the award added value and prestige. *Whatever It Takes* also signified in a specific way the larger company ethic: no matter how big we got, we still treated people as important individuals. It's why we didn't refer to stores by their numbers.

Several times each year, I'd host a conference call with all our store managers that I labeled *State of the rueUnion*. It was one of the ways I worked hard to give our fast-growing company the intimate feel of a small company. With 1,500 store associates on the line, we would give a shout-out to a select few to highlight worthy achievements.

I like to keep things simple within the company, so they don't spin out of control. You never want to lose touch with what's going on out in the field.

An important part of the corporate culture at rue21 was professional development. It's not how many people you have, but the quality of those people.

To recruit future associates, we ran an *Intern Mentorship* program. Each year from May to August, we'd hire up to fifteen college students who were on summer break. They were young, bright, and ambitious, the best workers to train. Our management team enjoyed having them on board. They were assigned to departments across the company, in merchandising, planning, finance, marketing, human resources, and store operations. They were full of inventive ideas, from creating apps to suggesting flextime schedules. One-third of the interns came back after graduation to work for us.

We had several programs to support and encourage the growth of associates. We groomed hand-picked people who had the potential to be managers and assistant managers for management advancement development (MAD). In addition, we ran a training program for all field associates called *rueniversity*.

Our *SOS* team of store opening specialists helped ensure that store managers and district managers were totally prepared to successfully open new locations. We got it down to such a science, a store could be opened in six weeks. We never missed a scheduled store opening date.

I took pride during my fifteen years at rue21 in creating an intern *Mentoring* program to support job advancement through personal development. I enjoy seeing the potential in people and working with them to help them fulfill that potential. In fact, there's nothing I like better than seeing a person achieve success and happiness.

That's why I value and keep in touch with my past experiences, from day one at A&S, all the way through day 15,805 at rue21. I don't want to lose the feeling of what it is like to be in the trenches, trying to get ahead, figuring out how to work smarter to improve my numbers.

Teaching *Millennials* business while they teach me life is *Mutual Mentoring* at its best.

# CHAPTER FOUR

# TRIBAL KNOWLEDGE

**When a company changes its CEO, the incoming executive often is brought in to shake things up.** That was the situation when I arrived at rue21 in the summer of 2001.

I needed people with the right credentials in the right positions. I wasted no time sizing up the management staff.

**Dione Odell** wasn't part of senior management. She was an assistant manager. I learned about her through a senior manager, who made some critical comments to me about Dione.

I know there are two sides to every story, and I was curious to hear what Dione had to say. At my first meeting with her, I could tell right away she was **Genuine**. Here was a **Dedicated Worker** who conveyed to me, in her own unassuming way, that she had the company's best interests in mind. As I listened to her, I could tell she didn't limit herself by her job description. She took control and did whatever was required to exceed expectations. Associates like that are gold to me: I never take them for granted.

*Genuine* and *Dedicated* are two of the chief characteristics of *Tribal Knowledge*. People who fit that description don't brag about what they can do, don't blame others if something goes wrong, and get the job done quietly, efficiently, and well.

Dione Odell is the kind of model worker who epitomizes the value of *Tribal Knowledge*.

I'm a big believer in *Tribal Knowledge*. I have found it to be a reliable judge of character, so much so that I attribute much of my business success to it.

*Tribal Knowledge* is not based on theory. Wishful thinking isn't part of it either. It's also *not* paper knowledge; you won't find it on a resume.

*Tribal Knowledge* is based on authentic wisdom that accumulates over time, from experience. It requires a strong work ethic. It feeds on solid information and intangibles. It's organic, as in hard-won knowledge; it's not synthetic, as in assumed or imagined knowledge.

People who create the pulse and who feed off the pulse of an organization are the energy source of *Tribal Knowledge*. They are loyal to the company's goals and its pursuit of excellence. Along with their dedication comes an implicit trust in the leadership. They know how to build a business.

Someone with *Tribal Knowledge* who uses it effectively may be an overachiever, or a late bloomer, or a self-made success story. *Tribal Knowledge* can help people overcome long odds or break through big obstacles. They don't draw attention to themselves. They don't wear their credentials like medals. Their inherent value to the company can be measured not in academic honors or industry awards, but in sweat equity.

# TRIBAL
# KNOWLEDGE

The pedigree of a big-name company or college is nice, but **give me anybody with**

# STREET
# SMARTS
# PASSION AND
# PRACTICAL
# EXPERIENCE
# WHO WORKS HARD

AND I'LL GIVE YOU **GROWTH & PROFITS.**

## DON'T BE FOOLED BY "PEDIGREE"

In my career, I've seen that it's entirely possible to put together a very strong team from a diverse group of personalities who may not at first come off as the obvious or best choices for their roles.

They are not necessarily what some might think of as "pedigreed." They may not stand out in a crowd. They simply know what they are doing, go about their job methodically, and take pride in the quality of their work.

Most important, they are in touch with the needs of the customer, their coworkers, and their bosses. They are able to relate well to all of the constituencies who determine how successful they can become.

The same goes for how I used *Tribal Knowledge* to improve my chances of success and benefit the company. I enjoyed working with all kinds of people. I took the time, whenever I could, to talk with store associates and with customers.

My top priority is always what the customer wants, not what *I* think is cool. I was fortunate to build a company at rue21 filled with people in key positions who had *Tribal Knowledge*.

Whatever I accomplished at rue21 can be credited to them. I'm not saying people like that just fell into my lap by accident. Some had worked with me at past companies. Others were new discoveries.

*Tribal Knowledge* is an important part of who I am, and how I think, so I make it a point to look for others who have it when hiring or networking. You should too. Don't rely only on people you know, and already are comfortable with, to get the job done right.

There are people with *Tribal Knowledge* out there who may not immediately fit your idea of the ideal associate, based on, say, demographics. *Tribal Knowledge* is not always easy to find. It's not always evident in how a person looks, dresses, or speaks. First, learn how to spot it. Then, if it is within your grasp, don't let those people slip away. They will make you look better for hiring them.

Where pedigrees are valuable and impressive in theory, *Tribal Knowledge* is the practical application of our personal assets—what each of us brings to the table.

I want to be careful here, though, so there's no misunderstanding: *Tribal Knowledge* is not necessarily the absence of pedigree. The point is that it doesn't *rely* on pedigree to get the job done. It relies on ingenuity, backed by hard work, focus, and dedication. It relies on people who know how to make a difference. Those are the people I tap into first and foremost. They show me the way as much as I show them the way. It works best when it's a fully symbiotic relationship—once again, *Mutual Mentoring!*

## GREAT PLANS NEED GREAT PEOPLE

Companies with a good business plan and mediocre people don't make it. Companies with a good plan and good people do. *Companies with a great plan and great people become a business like rue21.*

> **Companies with a good business plan and mediocre people don't make it. Companies with a good plan and good people do.**

As happened during the holiday season of 2011, when rue21 gained ten percentage points in comp sales (in stores opened at least one year) within a couple of weeks. We both defied and exceeded expectations by all pulling in the same direction, harnessing the belief we had in each other to hit our numbers when we needed it most.

The part of my own *Tribal Knowledge* I rely on the most is reading people, understanding them, and pushing them to first envision, and then to reach, their own potential.

I don't claim to have a magic formula. I'm not saying I was born smarter than the next guy. I listen to what customers want and figure out how to give it to them at a fair value that enhances my bottom line.

It's not my style to insist there's only one way to do something—or else! My success, and that of the people I've surrounded myself with, is more the result of staying both unbiased and open-minded. Once I see an opportunity developing, I want to discover how to nurture it, and then how we can repeat that process to maintain *Momentum*.

My philosophy hinges on the belief that not everything in life or business can be reduced to simple black and white. So much of life is gray. You have to recognize and deal with that gray area.


## THE POWER OF PASSION

There is a singular ingredient of *Tribal Knowledge* I value the most: *Passion*.

That brings me back to Dione Odell. The best way to judge people, in my view, is not by writing an assessment of their per-formance and behavior. I evaluate people in the workplace every day and give them feedback right there, on the spot. That's using everyday *Tribal Knowledge* to judge performance rather than filling out a largely irrelevant form once a year.

A short time after I had met with Dione to hear her side of the senior manager's criticisms about her, her manager, who was in charge of the district managers, left the company. Her departure created a vacuum that I had to fill. Until I could find a replacement, I'd have to cover the position myself.

# DIG BENEATH THE DATA

In all my positions as a CEO through the years, I worked hard at accumulating as much information as I could to guide my decisions. Understanding how things work in every corner of the company makes you a smarter manager who can make better decisions. It immerses you in the collective **Tribal Knowledge** of the entire company.

Information is more than data. It includes intangibles that don't show up in hard numbers. It's not always about such standard performance metrics as revenue per square foot or other spreadsheet statistics. I relish knowing the intangibles that make a store a success or an underperformer.

To get at that hidden information, you have to read between the lines. It is not standard practice for most CEOs, but I made it a point to play an active role in each meeting about stores we were planning to open or close. I made a commitment to shareholders that I'd be involved in every detail, not just rely on data sheets.

Don't let data be your only guide to making the best decisions. There's always more to the story that you need to know. Maybe it's true that numbers don't lie. But they don't always tell the whole truth either.

Clearly, it was not a good situation for me or for the district managers who were used to a set routine, receiving their marching orders on a weekly conference call. It was a routine I had not participated in, yet here I was trying to figure out how I was going to manage this new challenge on top of all my other corporate responsibilities.

Then I received unexpected information.

I was in my office with Dione. With her former boss now gone, I was picking her brain about the best way for me to handle the conference call.

Dione looked at me, as if to say, "What are you talking about?" It turned out that she had been running the show all along. She laughed at my thinking that her former boss was the one who handled the conference calls.

Dione then did her thing, speaking to the district managers for an hour.

When I complimented her on her mastery of managing the call and the district managers, she was very cool about it: "No big deal," she assured me, adding that was how she always orchestrated the Monday meeting.

That's why Dione embodies my ideal of *Tribal Knowledge*. She knew just what to do and she went about doing it without any fanfare. It's a tribute to her fortitude that she had stuck it out as long as she had before I got to rue21.

Dione had something else she wanted to tell me. What most interested her—*her Passion*—was marketing, not store operations. She moved over to that department, starting as an assistant. She didn't have a degree in marketing, or any formal training for that category. Nothing was going to stop her from fulfilling her *Passion*.

Capitalizing on her *Tribal Knowledge*, Dione kept to it, rising through the ranks over time to become VP of marketing. As much as

## YOU CAN GO YOUR OWN WAY, OR ...

People with **Tribal Knowledge** carve their own path in the world. They may not be the smoothest (or fastest) talkers, but the value they bring is more essential than slick optics: it's substance and **Passion**.

Those who possess **Tribal Knowledge** don't try to dazzle with fancy footwork. They move with focus and with purpose in a straight line. They deliver results reliably by doing **Whatever It Takes**.

It's hard to do that alone, though. That's why having a **Mentor** is vital.

I like to help people figure out how they can make the most of their abilities and instincts. A **Mentor** can't create instincts, but can help refine them.

Sometimes it means holding the person's feet to the fire, pushing him or her hard toward the goal line. I **Mentored** Dione Odell, who went from having shaky confidence when speaking in front of people to becoming a self-assured star in the company.

Whether you are the **Mentor** or the one being **Mentored**, the key is to harness the passion and instincts already there to help both them and the company.

Who is your Dione you can help with **Mentoring**?

Or, are *you* a Dione who has the potential and needs to find a **Mentor**?

anyone, she was an integral part of building rue21. Dione to this day is a trusted confidante whose opinions and friendship I greatly value.

With people like Dione Odell to strengthen my hand, I knew, in that moment, I was going to make it. I can control merchandising and marketing, but it's crazy to expect a CEO to be hands-on day to day with 255 stores and thirty district managers. That's where the chain of command needs to kick in.

The top executive's job is to hire good people, empower them, lead them, and create a corporate culture that supports and rewards their efforts. If it's done any other way—if a CEO gets too far into the weeds with line managers—a company can get dysfunctional very quickly.

If it wasn't for Dione, I simply would have had to dive deeper to add another layer to my own *Tribal Knowledge*.

## rue21 STORES AS VIDEO STARS

We had a standing practice at rue21 for all newly opened stores to produce their own video. I had a couple of reasons for the video policy: I had told investors that as long as I was in charge at rue21, I would always review stores firsthand. It also was a great way for me to get to know a little bit about the associates working in each store long before I would have a chance to visit each location in person. (During our growth spurt, we averaged two store openings every week.)

The videos soon took on a life of their own, and the support center staff looked forward to receiving and watching each one. It became a special event, like a viewing party. The people who produced them were young, working in underserved markets, and without a lot of experience creating an important presentation like this that would be scrutinized by the top bosses at the home office.

They were excited about opening a store, and went all out to impress us, while having fun at the same time. Besides, the videos served as a glitzy showcase for their *Tribal Knowledge*. It was a great motivational tool that produced great results.

The staff of a store in Owensboro, Kentucky, created a video that impressed me so much, I played it at ICR, a major industry conference for investors. The audience loved it. The video used the catchy opening theme music from the classic TV sitcom *Green Acres*, and it showed the store associates poking good-natured fun at their farm lifestyle. I even brought in one of the video "stars" for a managers' meeting in our support center as an example of the rue21 culture working its magic in the heartland of America.

Over a ten-year period, we opened one thousand stores. By watching about eight hundred videos of those openings, I was able to virtually "meet" the store managers and associates, and to get a better feel for the local culture. People from all divisions of the company were required to attend the viewings.

When problems in the store were evident in the video, it was painful for them to confront the issue. Yet that was part of the point of the video. After the video ended, I would ask, "What action did you take in that store to fix the problem?" We usually learned something new from the videos that could help us improve other stores as well. Watching them was a worthwhile educational experience. It expanded our *Tribal Knowledge* of rue21 stores that were hundreds or thousands of miles from us.

In some cases, I would call the store manager to thank him or her for making the video. All of them showcased the pride of the rue associates, and the culture we nurtured, which our customers felt when they shopped in our stores.

Whenever I spoke with store managers, I would say, "We only have one store right now—your store." That also put pressure back on them to be accountable, as if they owned the store. I would ask them, "What would you change about the store?" It all comes down to how you are able to get the people in charge to respond to you. I did it, in part, by asking questions that caused them to look at things the same way as did the person with ultimate responsibility—me. More than that, I told the manager, "Look at the store like you're a customer."

You would have thought the people working in our stores owned the stores. That's how much pride they took in being part of the rue21 family.

To underscore that pride, the videos always would end with our rallying cry, "Do you rue? I do!"

## STAY CURIOUS

One of the keys to *Tribal Knowledge* is curiosity.

At the ICR conference, I rarely saw CEOs attending presentations by other retailers, even if it was a direct competitor. More often than not, I was the only one who did that. I was curious about what they had to say and how the audience reacted to it. To not take advantage of that opportunity would mean I'm operating in a vacuum. You also never know when you might pick up some good ideas along the way. That's right: *Tribal Knowledge* is transferable. It can be used in different companies or different industries. That's what makes it such a valuable commodity.

There are times when you come by *Tribal Knowledge* under what could be the most unimaginable circumstances. One of the members of the *Fisch Tales Millennial Advisory Board* tells an

# TREAT EACH LINK LIKE IT'S THE ONLY LINK

As the term implies, a retail chain is made up of many links, or stores. Sure, they all are connected in various ways, but my philosophy is to treat each store like it's my only store.

I don't make assumptions about other stores based on the performance of one store. Even though it's part of a retail chain, each store is unique in other ways, with its own culture and set of circumstances. Where is it located? What other stores are around it? Who is on staff? What is the makeup of the local population? Those all are part of the mix.

Even if I'm opening as many as 100 stores a year—which is exactly what we did at rue21 for a full decade—each store is as important to me as if we were opening just one store a year.

That's a valuable lesson in any business or area of life. Don't skim the surface. Don't make assumptions based on general knowledge about your business.

Dig deep to treat each situation as one-of-a-kind. Remember, the big picture consists of little pictures that are connected to the whole, but in other ways also have a life of their own, independent of each other. That's what **Tribal Knowledge** is all about.

intensely personal story of what it was like to volunteer in New York City in the horrific aftermath of the 9/11 collapse of the World Trade Center towers. It's a good reminder that a byproduct of self-sacrifice is *Tribal Knowledge*. Acknowledging the hardships of others and doing what you can to lighten their load develops empathy. Connecting instinctively with others is a prized quality you can use productively in other situations, whether it's business or personal. It is clearly a sign of a good manager, but also of a good coworker and team player. Tribe and team are synonymous.

Teamwork fuels *Tribal Knowledge*. It ties everything together in a way that makes everyone succeed. It's finding purpose in your work without merely going through the motions.

As our *Millennial Advisory Board* points out, "Your wealth is defined by your experience." Words to live (and thrive) by.

As it grew to become the largest US specialty apparel retailer by store count, rue21 proved to be a model of how far *Tribal Knowledge* can take a company.

rue21 used its *Tribal Knowledge* to go where others feared to tread, and we won the day by following that strategy. We put together a trifecta of fashion, quality, and value in underserved markets throughout the country. The further we reached into the suburbs and away from the cities, the less rent we paid, the more sales we achieved, and the more profit we made. That became the surefire model for rue21's success in strip centers and value malls, where we felt comfortably at home, as customers flocked to fill our stores and our cash registers.

## COMIN' ROUND THE MOUNTAIN

One of the proudest and most amazing days for me at rue21 took place in a rue store in November 2014. This wasn't just any store. It epitomized what made us different from all other retailers, and what made us a fan favorite in the markets we served.

As part of treating each store as if it were our only store, I always insisted we not refer to them by store number. This store was our Logan, West Virginia, store.

I was with my management team on day two of a road trip. The Logan store had opened the day before. Visiting each store wasn't like the movie, *Groundhog Day*; each one was a new experience. We never knew exactly what to expect.

So, there we were, rounding the side of the mountains of West Virginia, overlooking a cliff, and craning our necks to catch a glimpse of the Walmart Supercenter, near where the two-day-old rue store was located. Suddenly, out of nowhere, a lonely strip center came into view, like an oasis in the desert.

We instantly were dumbstruck at the sight of the Walmart Supercenter parking lot chock full of vehicles. In this town of fifteen thousand, with the closest shopping center sixty miles away, it was as if everyone in Logan, West Virginia, decided to shop at the local Walmart at the same time!

That was not an encouraging sign. We began to worry, fearing that some of the people who had come to shop at rue might get frustrated at the difficulty finding a parking spot and leave without visiting the store.

After pulling into the lot, we began to feel a little better at the sight of the town's high school football team handing out flyers in front of the new rue.

After walking into the store, the management team and I went from feeling a little better to being blown away by the incredible scene. In the rue store, packing the aisles from wall to wall, were probably 150 energized customers of all ages, some filling shopping carts they had brought over from Walmart!

Locals were lined up at the nearby bank to get cash for their purchases.

Despite its limited customer base, without another shopping center within sixty miles, the Logan store became our top store in sales that December and rue's top store overall in that year's fourth quarter.

When we arrived, the manager of the store said it was an honor to meet the CEO of rue. I replied to her that "the honor is meeting you and your store team." I know that sounds like two people just exchanging pleasantries, but I meant every word.

After spending time in the store observing and interacting with the associates, I saw how much they were totally in the pulse of their community and their customers. They came to work each day eager to do **Whatever It Takes** to help the company succeed. All of that is what *Tribal Knowledge* is all about!

The trip to Logan was a defining moment for me, not only at rue but in my entire four-decade-plus career in retailing. People in the store were coming up to me like I had just emerged from the stage door of a hit Broadway show after a performance. It was a heady feeling.

Appreciating and putting faith in *Genuine* people with *Tribal Knowledge* like the Logan team is why rue was a one-of-a-kind experience—for me, for my management team, for the store associates, and for our customers.

It also made me realize that, for our customers, the rue shopping experience had the power to change people's lives in many underserved, smaller towns.

The Logan store opening was greeted as a major event. Creating something that gave back to that community created an immense sense of pride. You had to be there to believe it, and I'm forever grateful that I was there to see it and feel it.

"Do you rue? I do!"

And I always will.

# CHAPTER FIVE

# BOB'S CLUB IS NO BOYS' CLUB

**The sexual revolution that *Baby Boomers* grew up in, during the 1960s, was about *freedom* of sexual expression.** The sexual revolution of the new *Millennium* is about *suppression* of inappropriate sexual expression that is not consensual, which is another way of saying it is uninvited or unwanted.

We go through cycles, which is fine. It's all part of life's learning process.

The #MeToo backlash against mistreatment of women has a different intensity among *Millennials*. Some of my *Millennial Advisory Board* members, who've been in the workforce for a decade or so at most, haven't experienced nearly as much sexism at work as *Gen X* or *Baby Boomer* females. They tend to be in general agreement that the level of tolerance a woman should have for fielding a remark (or an advance) made by someone other than a partner varies with each situation—it depends on context.

If you imply that a person's looks influenced your hiring decision, in most cases, that would be viewed as offensive.

If you compliment a person's new hairstyle or choice of wardrobe in a tasteful manner, that, on the face of it, would not be offensive.

I'm not saying that there is unanimous agreement on how either of those remarks would be perceived. At the same time, I would like to think we can find reasonable room to accept workplace comments that are innocent and well intended.

## GENDER-BLIND

Long before the #MeToo movement built up a healthy head of steam, I never viewed women in business as anything other than workers first. To a large degree, anyone's gender to me is incidental. It doesn't determine what I think of a person, whether it's in the workplace or elsewhere.

I don't see gender as a sign of competence or work ethic. Treating women differently from men based on gender is foolish. I wouldn't do that. I never have.

If I lean slightly more in one direction than the other, I tend to trust female instincts more than I do male instincts. There were men on my management team who, at times, became jealous when I spent more time with female executives than I did with their male counterparts.

The characteristics often criticized in women at work are, ironically, what I think make them more effective workers. If some of the female merchants on my team were quicker to become emotional, that was fine with me. I admire passion in people.

Retail is a tough business; releasing emotion is a form of therapy. It doesn't mean you're not tough. It means you care about the work you are doing, and about the results you are getting.

In the office culture, women often are less political than men. And certain triggers can more easily provoke a man's temper. Those tendencies can work against making the best decisions. They can disrupt the camaraderie of the team, which undermines productivity.

Here's one example of what I mean.

A member of our *Millennial Advisory Board, Nicole Campbell*, told me how a group of males reacted to an initiative called *Ladies Get Paid*. It was formed to "give women the tools and resources they need to rise up at work."

*Ladies Get Paid* also encourages more diversity at the management level. The name is derived from the glaring contrast in pay scales between men and women, an inequality that is the most obvious form of sexism in the workplace. It is common knowledge that women have historically been paid less than their male counterparts.[1]

For that reason alone, I think it's great that there are female activist groups like *Ladies Get Paid*. They're long overdue. Here's the part I don't get: Nicole told me *Ladies Get Paid* had been sued by a group of men for discriminatory practices!

## DO MEN FEAR A LEVEL PLAYING FIELD?

Sounds like a bad joke. Instead, it's a sad fact that there are plenty of men who think that way. The only explanation is that they are afraid of a level playing field with the opposite sex. My advice to them is:

---

1   "The State of the Gender Pay Gap 2019," PayScale, https://www.payscale.com/data/gender-pay-gap.

"Deal with it!"

When I run a business, I see and treat men and women as equals. As mentioned in chapter 4, when it comes to capability and performance, a person's *Tribal Knowledge* is much more important to me than gender.

The same goes for physical appearance. Other than having reasonable expectations of men and women dressing in a professional, presentable manner, a person's looks or taste in clothes should not weigh heavily when judging a candidate's competence.

Personality is another matter, though. It *is* important. In the business of retailing, it's an advantage to be outgoing. If you want to be "heard" and valued for your opinions, you must speak up and *Take a Stand.*

A big part of what I enjoy about *Mentoring* is helping those who need to work on their persona in order to have their voice heard. Being able to project your personality and your force of will to others you work with is known as *Amplification.*

## FROM *MAD MEN* TO EMPOWERED WOMEN

For a long time, women in the workplace typically were discouraged from speaking up among male colleagues. Just look at cult TV drama *Mad Men.* It showed how the chauvinistic culture of Madison Avenue advertising agencies in the 1960s kept a glass ceiling intact. Talented women struggled to compete for influential and better-paying positions controlled exclusively by men.

I'm proud to be part of the *Millennial* era, which empowers females, as I do, encouraging them to take control. Women in my companies definitely did not have an *Amplification* problem. Everyone knew where the female managers stood and knew what

## PERSONA VERSUS PERSONALITY

It takes all kinds of personalities to make a company succeed. Obviously, no manager should try to change someone's personality to fit in with others. If the person is skilled enough to keep on board, but difficult to work with, that's a behavioral issue that you try to work out.

Someone's persona, however, is a different story. A persona can be developed to help someone communicate and relate better with colleagues. A persona is not always a precise mirror of personality; a persona may in fact mask it.

I've worked closely with people to help them solidify a persona. By pushing people to do things for me they didn't think they could do, I'm also pushing them to sharpen and broaden their persona. That way, they develop a reputation for being versatile by tackling a variety of challenges.

It's important to be aware of how people perceive you. It's perfectly OK to have a personality that is shy or soft spoken. What's not OK is to let it hold you back from speaking up for yourself, for your ideas, and for your accomplishments.

those managers expected of others who reported to them.

It wasn't uncommon for male executives on my team to be challenged—even intimidated—by the dominant women in our midst. My advice to those men, again, was: Deal. With. It.

There were times when it wasn't pretty. A submissive male easily could be chewed up like chopped meat. I had no problem with that; for those men, it was a learning experience. It also worked to the advantage of our business for female managers to push their agenda aggressively.

I would tell people who worked for me to keep pushing and not *take "no"* for an answer to get what they wanted. Many times, it was the women who outran the men in that respect, and their positive and persistent attitude helped our business take off. I love people who are relentless in getting what they want. I easily relate to them because I'm the same way.

# BE A TEAM PLAYER, NOT A PRIMA DONNA

A senior executive at rue21 who had been with us for a month once left the building without telling anyone of his whereabouts. He wasn't prepared, upon his return to the office, to be chewed out by a female VP.

***Judy Kucinski*** kept an eye on everyone. She did it to benefit the company's productivity. It is a good thing when you have someone like her who cares so much.

After being lectured by Judy for going momentarily AWOL, the male C-suite executive complained to me: "I don't have to tell her where I am."

I took him aside and explained how we worked at rue21: gender doesn't matter. Neither does your rank in the company pecking order. We work as a team at all times. No prima donnas—and no primo uomos.

In any company, survival of the fittest rules. To complain that someone beneath your management level is giving you a hard time is really bad optics. You're whining about who someone is, which has nothing to do with the person's competence or contribution to the business. Pull your weight, and pull in the same direction as everyone else, and you'll get the respect you deserve.

# CHAPTER SIX

# THE DISRUPTOR

**I've always prided myself on being a *Disruptive* force in my professional life.** That attitude applies to my personal life too. I have no regrets about playing it my way because the results have been gratifying, not only to me, but to others who've benefited from those results.

One of the traits that makes me a born *Disruptor* is that I always have had a hard time going with the flow. Going against the flow usually is where you'll find fresher solutions and fewer competitors—both personally and corporately. It's always been my style to do the unexpected, to go against the grain.

Sometimes playing *Disruptor* requires you to respond boldly to an event outside your control.

That's what happened to me in 2011 at rue21, when a cotton crisis ripped through the apparel industry, and effectively changed

# DISRUPTOR

## MEANS BEING AN INNOVATOR, THE PROVERBIAL MOVER & SHAKER.

DISRUPTORS
**BLAZE NEW TRAILS**

BY GOING
**AGAINST THE FLOW.**

BY DEFINITION,
**THEY ARE IN THE MINORITY.**

the business for years to come. Due to a shortage, cotton suppliers were forced to raise the prices they charged retail accounts. Retailers believed they had no choice but to pass along the increased costs to their customers.

Did we raise our prices at rue21 like the other retailers reflexively did? Of course not. That strategy made no sense to me. Even today, the effects of that crisis are being felt in retail. Now, the focus is on promotional pricing for its own sake, instead of on the value of merchandise.

Dealing with change is not easy for most people, but the ordeal of making adjustments sharpens your skills, leads to discovery, and creates new opportunities.

I know that *Disruption* at first sounds destructive, something you want to avoid. Get rid of that negative thought. To the contrary, when used properly, *Disruption* is a powerful and underestimated tool of creativity and productivity.

If things are not working the way you need them to work, what choice do you have, other than to *Disrupt* the status quo? That's what every great inventor, artist, and business innovator in the history of the world has done. They *Take a Stand* and *Put It on the Line*, no matter how much resistance or skepticism greets their intentions and actions.

## "I MAKE YOU EMPEROR!"

I've had the privilege of working with some of the most powerful merchants in the world, including people like *Leonardo Del Vecchio* (known in the business by his initials, LDV, or simply as "Mr. Del Vecchio").

# IT'S DISRUPTORS AGAINST THE WORLD

Being a **Disruptor** means being an innovator, the proverbial mover and shaker. **Disruptors** blaze new trails by going against the flow. By definition, then, they are in the minority.

Everybody else falls into one of two camps: There are the interrupters. They get in the way of the **Disruptors** for one reason or another.

It may be competitive, with both vying to move up the corporate ladder when only one position is open. Or the interrupter may be a contrarian with a "not invented here" stubborn streak.

Both the **Disruptor** and the interrupter are activists.

The other, and most common, type of person in this scenario is the passive bystander. Rather than rock the boat, bystanders are content to hang back, watch the **Disruptors** and interrupters duke it out, and then go with the flow, riding the coattails of whoever prevails. They are the opposite of risk-takers.

In short, the **Disruptor** acts, the interrupter reacts, the bystander spectates.

If you're content to be anything other than a **Disruptor**, this book isn't for you, so you may as well stop reading right here. But I know you'll keep reading because if you weren't a **Disruptor**, you wouldn't have read this far.

In 1995, I was president of retailer Casual Corner when the formidable LDV took over the parent company. He told me that my new title would be business manager. True to the American fixation on the importance of job titles, my ego couldn't imagine going from president to business manager, and I told Mr. Del Vecchio so.

In this case, I really wasn't trying to be *Disruptive*, but LDV sure saw it that way.

I was not prepared for what happened next. To my shock, his face became beet red and his neck veins started to bulge, as he shouted at me, "I make you emperor!" In that moment, I wondered if I'd be fired. I wasn't.

In one sense, he was joking, but in a more real sense, he didn't intend what he said to be funny. Mr. Del Vecchio was genuinely angry, and he was making a point I never would forget.

The point is to respect the habits and behavior of your surroundings, and then follow suit. Europeans had bought our company, so I learned to become more receptive and responsive to their style of management. In this case, unlike Americans in business, Europeans aren't obsessed with the title on your business card. It was a humbling, as well as a learning, experience. I came to recognize that the European way made sense.

Leonardo Del Vecchio, a brilliant builder of businesses, was taking over our company and trying to right the ship. Who was I to question his decisions?

There's another lesson there: the American way is to think about yourself and your title. The European way is that a title is not as important as being the right leader, thinking about your people, and finding ways to drive the business to make money for the company.

It's all about entrepreneurship. Don't let a particular process stick you in a box that inhibits your behavior. Make the most of the resources you are given and work the process to your advantage, tweaking it along the way as necessary. You'll get what you want, whether you're called a business manager, president—or emperor!

(By the way, after Mr. Del Vecchio saw that his point landed as intended, he let me continue with the title of president.)

One of my proudest *Disruptor* moments took place in a men's restroom. (I know what you're thinking: talk about going against the flow!) This is a true story, so let me flush it—I mean *flesh* it—out for you.

## NOTHING'S OFF LIMITS

When I was a divisional merchandise manager in the 1990s at Jordan Marsh in Miami, I did not like to use the bathroom designated for my management level. There always were puddles on the floor and I wasn't about to risk getting my clothes wet by wading in there.

Without asking permission, I used the executive bathroom that was the exclusive domain of upper management.

By frequenting the executive washroom that technically was off limits to me, I had regular access to confidential sales reports that weren't circulated to people at my level.

By studying the reports, I was able to see how all the other Jordan Marsh divisions, outside of my dress business, were performing, and to compare our performance to theirs. It gave me valuable insight not only into my corner of the company but to the big picture.

The senior executives thought it was pretty ballsy of me to use their bathroom, but I didn't care if they thought I was arrogant. They even joked about it. That grudging respect told me that, behind their outward disdain for what I was doing, they admired my assertiveness in going outside the box.

When I advanced to their level after eighteen months on the job, the Jordan Marsh executive who promoted me said the resourcefulness I demonstrated in getting my hands on those confidential sales reports impressed him. He liked how I went out of my way to stay on top of my business, and at the same time stay fully informed about the entire store's performance.

Another way I didn't travel with the pack is how I handled performance reviews. People who worked for me knew that annual reviews were superfluous.

In some quarters of corporate America, people in charge of human resources love the 360-degree review. With that method, in addition to bosses evaluating associates, the associates also evaluate their bosses. I had no use for that type of review either. If I can't be passionate about it, I'm not going to waste everyone's time with it.

We spent $200,000 on a consulting firm that would ask our associates at rue21 questions like, "Does Bob micromanage you?" Some would say yes; some would say no.

I don't see why the term *micromanaging* should have a bad connotation. If I'm not managing, I'm not doing my job. Micro means you're sweating the details. You're doing your job by helping others succeed in their jobs.

They said I should review people at the end of the year. No! I reviewed people every day. I didn't want people in my company to spend six months making mistakes that I could help them correct in a day. My intervention worked very well for everyone concerned.

## CRISIS FOR OTHERS, OPPORTUNITY FOR US

There were two reasons we were able to weather the cotton crisis.

One reason is that rue21 did not buy directly from the offshore, brand-name vendors that sold to other chains, and now were charging

# DON'T CONFUSE ISSUES WITH LOGIC

One of my favorite pieces of advice to those I mentor is "Do not confuse issues with logic."

Simple logic would tell a retail CEO that a recession—namely, the one that affected the US from 2008–2009—is no time to aggressively expand. And that illustrates one of the problems with simple logic: It doesn't always take into account variables.

The business model I had envisioned for rue21 was as a *value* fashion retailer. We were exactly the kind of money-saving destination store that a teen or twenty-something consumer would shop in during a recession, when their budget, or their parents' budget, was especially tight.

When the recession started at the end of 2008, we were in the middle of adding stores at a furious clip of more than one a week. The recession continued until June of 2009, and so did our expansion, reaching 500 stores by then. That November, we doubled down on our confident growth plan by going out with a highly successful initial public offering.

None of that would have been possible if I had confused issues (store expansion) with logic (recession) by slowing our rate of growth.

A solution doesn't need to sound logical. It just needs to work. Make things happen!

higher prices during the shortage. Instead, we always purchased our inventory domestically, through off-brand importers. That strategy kept our costs low.

As one of the largest retail accounts for many of our vendors, we had a lot of clout, and we did not hesitate to use it. We held our ground with suppliers by telling them we could not pay more than we currently were paying.

That clout also worked for us down the line. When you're ordering a million pieces of an item at a time, as we did, your vendor can leverage that high volume to negotiate better prices with its sources. Because we dug in our heels, it worked out that no suppliers in our pipeline raised prices during the crisis.

As a result, we didn't have to jack up our retail prices, which stayed stable throughout the cotton crisis.

The second reason we bucked the higher-price trend is that I knew this was the ideal climate for us to go against the industry flow to capture additional market share from our competitors.

We told our vendors they should not overreact. We were confident that pricing levels would revert to their previous lower levels the following year. Sure enough, that's just what happened.

That's a good example of using your knowledge of how things worked out in the past under similar conditions to give you a firmer grasp of how to proceed, while minimizing risk.

Heading into the 2011 holiday sales season, other retailers panicked at the thought of raising prices on their customers.

To compensate, and create demand, top chains like *American Eagle*, *Abercrombie & Fitch*, *Aéropostale*, *Gap*, and others promoted deep discounts of 50 percent off the entire store. That meant they had to sell twice as many units just to maintain flat sales from the previous year's comparable (or "comp") numbers (year-over-year sales comparisons for store locations open at least one year).

As other retailers raised their prices, rue21's prices, which were already discounted, would look that much more appealing to consumers.

For other retailers, who gave up both market share and profit margins, the cotton crisis was lose-lose. For us, it was win-win. We were one of a handful of retailers nationwide that weren't hurt by the crisis.

We disrupted the conventional wisdom automatically followed by the other retailers to make sure the cotton crisis didn't *Disrupt* our business. Think of it as fighting destructive *Disruption* with constructive *Disruption*.

The impact of the 2011 cotton crisis proved far-reaching, however. It left a lasting scar on the entire retail apparel industry. With goods at point of sale suddenly more expensive, the door was wide open for bold off-price discounters to walk in, like *T.J.Maxx*, *Marshalls*, *Ross*, and others.

Those discounters' grab for market share forced full-price retailers to run ongoing promotions to stay competitive. That marketing strategy undercut their profit margins, and they weren't able to gain enough market share to make up the difference.

*For rue21, though, the best was yet to come.*

# CHAPTER SEVEN

# SHITTIN' A BRICK

**The cotton crisis of 2011 affected everyone in soft goods retailing, some more than others.** rue21 arguably was one of the very few retailers that escaped relatively unscathed from that devastating turn of events.

We weren't taking a hit at the cash register with less revenue per transaction. We were consistent as we stood by our everyday prices, while at the same time discounting key *volume-merchandise* categories. That way, we were able to maintain a healthy balance of value pricing and full-margin pricing.

I was confident we would come through the holiday season in good shape. That's the realistic "guidance" I gave to the financial community on my quarterly call with investment analysts at the end of November 2011. Nevertheless, investors remained nervous and dubious that we could achieve our results without raising prices or

## PREPARE, DON'T PANIC

Take advantage of your experience to guide your decision-making process. Bring your **Tribal Knowledge** into play. Whatever you do, do not panic! Yes, the world changes, but it also usually returns to its previous position.

Much about the business world and the world marketplace is cyclical. Position yourself to be in a position of strength when a course correction restores normalcy to your business.

Success belongs to those who dig in their heels and trust their instincts.

offering lower pricing across the board.

Their skepticism didn't faze me. I was comfortable assuring them that rue21 would ring up a strong holiday sales performance in both our profit plan and our comp store sales.

## LOOKING FOR A 10 PERCENT SOLUTION

During the pre-Christmas week of 2011, rue21's comp sales were down 10 percent from the same holiday period in 2010. Not where we wanted to be. Even so, thanks to more shopping days remaining than in the previous year's calendar, we were confident of recapturing about half of that lost business.

Even with the sales gains we foresaw, a negative number that late in the shopping season did not encourage members of my management team. They were nervous. I was not.

As noted elsewhere in the book, I am a big believer in the practice of *Putting It on the Line* to get what you want. There's no challenge—or reward—to playing it safe all day long, and avoiding risks, and you can't expect to gain a lot in return. You get out of it what you put into it. I poured myself, and my reputation, into everything I did.

That's worth thinking about in your own situation. Be honest with yourself: Do you go all out to get the results you want, or do you expect more in return than your effort justifies? If you are frustrated with the results you get, analyze what you can do differently to change that outcome.

So, what was the method to my madness in going against the grain in late December 2011? At that time, it looked for all the world like rue21's numbers were going to fall considerably short of what I had virtually guaranteed the Wall Street crowd in my guidance a month earlier.

Since my teen years, I've always loved crunching and analyzing numbers, trends, and patterns. It could be a weather forecast, or it could be figuring out which factors affect sales of junior dresses. I looked for ways to exploit those factors to drive my business.

In late December 2011, I was studying the number of shopping days that remained. For one, I saw it as a good sign that there was another weekend of shopping before Christmas Day, compared with the previous year.

There was more good news. I saw that teens—who made up a large portion of our customer base—would return to classes later than the prior year. The longer they were on vacation, the more time they had to spend money in our stores.

Even though our pre-Christmas comp sales were off by 10 percent, a gift arrived at the eleventh hour: in places like Texas and Florida, schools wouldn't be back in session for another week. I saw that as fantastic news for rue21.

I learned a valuable lesson when I was at Jordan Marsh Miami. We cut prices and promoted frantically at year-end to make numbers, without taking into account that there were additional shopping days in the holiday season.

Our sales ended down 8 percent, and I swore to myself never to do that again. Thanks to that humbling experience, thirty years later, at rue21, with the same calendar working to our advantage, I knew what *not* to do.

## THE 13TH MONTH

I learned many valuable lessons during my early career at A&S, including one about holiday sales. In retailing, the period between Christmas and New Year's Day is called "the 13th month." For teen

# BE THE BELIEVER-IN-CHIEF

There will be times when the person in charge—of a company, a staff, or a project—will think he or she is the only one who believes in the plan on the table. That's not paranoia. That's life when you are a bold leader! Like they say, it's lonely at the top. When those around you are skeptical, hesitant, or contrary, don't shrink from your position of strength. Be the motivator, the facilitator. By not standing up for what you believe will be the best plan of attack, you are letting down your team. They will benefit as much as you when you all reach the goal line together.

shoppers, that so-called extra "month" is when they are on vacation, a time when they are eager to shop and redeem gift cards and coupons.

With the right merchandise, you can drive extra transactions and see significant sales growth, essentially turning a single week into the equivalent of a month's worth of business. The sales bump could be as much as 50–70 percent over Christmas week business.

The key is to focus not on discounting but on "newness." Retailers used to do that at the end of the year, but they had stopped doing that around 2011. At rue21, we didn't stop; we would bring in new color palettes of fashion items and other key merchandise that we knew would move quickly.

My reading of the calendar proved prophetic. On Dec. 23, 2011, we had shaved the negative number to 7 percent, meaning we were coming closer to at least staying even with the previous year. By the time New Year's Day 2012 rolled around, rue21 had achieved our goal for comp store sales—*just as I had predicted.*

I wasn't a magician or psychic. I just knew, from doing my homework and from my experience, that customers can't resist the allure of "newness," and most retailers did not capitalize on that in the so-called 13th month. Instead of bringing in fresh merchandise, they relied solely on promoting existing inventory. I assured my management team we would be okay using the "newness" strategy, and our plan proved correct.

## PICKING UP 10 POINTS IN 10 DAYS

Over a span of ten days, we had picked up ten percentage points in comp sales, which is like taking a leap across the Grand Canyon and landing safely on the other side—a daredevil feat.

As excited as I was about the company's comeback sales performance, I wanted to save the good news for the moment when it would have maximum impact. That would be at the annual ICR conference, taking place a couple of weeks later in Miami.

ICR is a destination event, a meeting of the minds where public and private companies present to, and meet with, investors, analysts, and other retailers. It is one of the largest and most prestigious investor conferences of the year.

To call this a critical audience for any major company is an understatement. The people who go to this conference, with their ears to the ground and their eyes on the prize, can make or break a stock price—along with a CEO's reputation—faster than you can say NASDAQ.

I had the choice of updating our holiday sales guidance either prior to the ICR conference or in my presentation during the conference, while standing in front of several hundred of America's most influential analysts.

I already had asked the conference organizer to give me a prime spot in the lineup. When I told **Joe Teklits**, managing partner of ICR, that I wanted to follow superstar retailer *Lululemon* on the program, he looked at me like I had lost my mind.

Lululemon was the darling of Wall Street handicappers. My eagerness to follow Lululemon on stage at ICR was like an unknown, new singer eagerly raising her hand to perform right after Lady Gaga. What sane person would ask to be put in that risky and vulnerable position? I would!

My rationale was simple: If you follow Lululemon, you make lemonade! Lululemon was the number-one retailer in the country, and it was leading off the conference, which meant it would have the largest audience of the event. I was happy to jump on Lululemon's

SCHOOL OF FISCH LESSON

# YOU'RE THE EXPERT!

The more experience you acquire in your field, the more you realize there are a lot of self-titled "experts" out there who don't know any more than you do. More often, they know less.

I am speaking not of hands-on practitioners who have direct experience in running the kind of business they are advising others about. I am thinking of people in the financial markets who handicap companies. As often as not, they can get it wrong.

Keep that in mind the next time you face a daunting situation and consider avoiding it for fear of an unwanted outcome. Don't be deterred by "experts" who haven't walked in your shoes. They may be desk jockeys who study data and make false conclusions based on that information.

Make believe you're at the beach, want badly to go for a swim, but know that the water is cold. Wading in slowly only makes it worse. Instead, you race to the water and, without overthinking it, dive right in. It's invigorating in a way that will open your eyes and your mind to new possibilities.

coattails and inherit that audience for my presentation.

That's the kind of challenge I look forward to. That's the kind of marquee moment I crave. If I'm not *Putting It on the Line*, I don't feel the full vitality of life that gets me moving. I need that extra burst to reach the next level of achievement.

## GO BIG OR GO HOME

I knew fully that I was taking a big chance in telling Joe I wanted to follow Lululemon. At the time I said that, our comp sales were down 10 percent, and our stock was underperforming.

Given those circumstances, it might have made more sense for me to instead seek a lower profile at the conference, in hopes I could slip out of there almost unnoticed. But, remember my advice from chapter 6: don't confuse issues with logic! Knowing I had that high-profile speaking slot was, by design, added motivation for me to make those numbers.

Our stock, which had peaked at $37.50 in 2011, by year-end had dipped to about half that price, below $20. My chief financial officer said, "We're done, we're finished." I knew better and told him to chill out, that we'd be fine. My CFO had a habit of becoming overly dramatic, and I would immediately snap him out of it.

As the 2012 ICR conference got underway, I wasn't commanding a great deal of respect. That world revolves around "What have you done for me lately?" Respect is doled out in direct proportion to your stock price. In fact, I could have driven a bulldozer through the conference, and nobody would have paid much attention. I was about to change that. My bulldozer was the surprising numbers in my hip pocket that nobody expected to hear.

## THE GOLD BRICK

Prominent investors in attendance at ICR were convinced that our holiday numbers were in the tank. The day before my 8:30 a.m. presentation, one of those investors, **Frank Alonso** of *T. Rowe Price,* said to Joe Teklits, "If Bob Fisch makes his guidance, *I'll shit a gold brick.*" I am not joking. Those were his exact words.

Little did Frank know that rue21 had made its guidance on the heels of the come-from-behind rally that we had staged heading into Jan. 1, 2012.

My management team and I were scheduled to have dinner that evening with Joe. As luck would have it, by sheer coincidence, he asked me if it was okay for Frank to join us.

I simply could have told Frank at dinner that we in fact had met the guidance I had given, and that he could spare himself the gold brick. But I did not want to divulge my numbers to another analyst who was going to be at the dinner table.

I could have let Frank find out the next morning, as he sat in the audience, along with five hundred others, and heard the bombshell news that nobody saw coming.

Neither of those options, though, was nearly as much fun as what I had in mind. Here was my *golden* opportunity to have some fun at Frank's expense. I figured turnabout is fair play, since his "shit a gold brick" prediction was made at my expense.

I went into overdrive to execute my plan—actually, it was my prank. At ten in the morning on the day of the dinner (the day before my presentation), I contacted my miracle worker of an executive assistant, **Dawn O'Brien**, in our Pittsburgh support center.

I told Dawn that I needed immediately a piece of chocolate packaged like a gold brick. Dawn did **Whatever It Takes**. By the time we sat down to dinner at ICR, I had in my hands a gold brick (of solid chocolate) to present to Frank, allowing him to make good on his promise to "shit a gold brick."

If I gave it to him at the table in front of everyone, with the other analyst present, it would ruin my surprise for the next morning.

In the middle of dinner, Frank excused himself from the table. I rose to accompany him. On our way to the men's room, I ceremoniously presented him with a beautifully wrapped package. He opened it to see a chocolate gold brick.

He was taken aback, exclaiming, "Oh, shit!" I reminded him what he said to Joe about shitting a gold brick. I didn't have to say one word more.

Frank was a good sport and we both laughed about it before returning to the table. There, members of my management team wore big smiles, as if to say, "We made it!" as each of them held up a small chocolate gold brick to show Frank.

At 8:30 the next morning, I took my place at the podium after Lululemon's CEO had completed her talk. Predictably, as was usual for the juggernaut chain, her report to the analysts and investors was very bullish.

What could I possibly say to match her crowd-pleasing performance?

## THE VIEW FROM CLOUD 9

PIECE OF THE PUZZLE

**ICR**
PRESENTATION

I didn't want to rush into the good news. Retailing is theater and I wanted to dramatize our accomplishment. I started my remarks by saying, "If I wasn't going to achieve guidance, I would tell you right now that I made a mistake. I was prepared to tell you that—if need be."

Savoring the moment, I teased out the unexpected news: "Well, many of you were wrong."

I explained that the cotton crisis did not cause rue21 to raise our retail prices and we did not slash prices through promotions. The net effect, I told them, was that rue21 sales and profit had rebounded to healthy levels. "I am proud and happy to report that, because of our prudent planning, we also will be achieving our sales plans."

After those words spilled out of my mouth, it was like a dam had burst. Investors flooded out of the room to signal to their brokers a "buy" recommendation on rue21 shares. As a result, our stock shot up to $25 from its previous $19.75, an extraordinary leap of 20 percent virtually overnight.

It wasn't just our stock that shot up like a rocket. That day, rue21 moved the entire stock market. We demonstrated that there was light at the end of the dark tunnel that was the cotton crisis.

It was quite a journey. More like a safari through a dangerous jungle. Starting in November 2011, when I first gave my December guidance, through the mid-January 2012 reiteration at ICR of the same guidance, I had *Put It on the Line* like I never had before.

If we did not make the guidance, I still would be locked into that presentation slot after Lululemon. Having to hang my head in shame would not have been pretty, but I would have owned up to it. Thankfully, that was not the case.

My number two, *Kim Reynolds*, the head merchant who had been by my side for thirty-plus years, couldn't get over that I had chosen to walk such a dangerous tightrope, let alone that I somehow had made it across the abyss while keeping my balance the whole way.

Kim was great at her job, with an in-your-face style that got results. Her brash personality is typical hard-charging Brooklynite:

she moves fast, talks fast, works fast, and doesn't sugarcoat anything.

That explains why one of my proudest moments occurred when the same Kim Reynolds, who was not quick to pat people on the back, told me, "You have the biggest balls I've ever seen to take that big a risk, and to end up there [on the podium], being able to say that."

The cloud over rue21—and the rest of the market—had started to lift. Our stock price now was on the way to $30 a share. My calculated risk paid off in a reversal of fortune for our stock, which had a positive effect on the whole market.

I went from the outlier with the hipster wardrobe to the golden boy. Suddenly, everyone wanted to get my opinion on business going forward. The following year, they sought assurances that I wasn't going to change what I had done the year before.

At the end of that eventful day at ICR, I watched the sun set at 5:30 p.m. while on the phone telling **Lynne Lindley**, a key member of my management team, that rue21 had "moved the market" with my blockbuster guidance announcement.

"This has been one of the most amazing days of my life," I said to her.

I was sitting on the terrace of my room at the FontaineBleau Hotel in Miami Beach, where the conference took place, and it felt as if I was floating on cloud nine.

I didn't just happen to luckily land on cloud nine. I made it my business to work my way up there, one career ladder rung at a time.

# CHAPTER EIGHT

# FROM LITTLE GUY TO MARKET MOVER

**In the early 1990s, value retailing was the new secret sauce for corporations like Casual Corner parent *US Shoe Corp*.** Casual Corner was one of the pioneers, blazing new ground. We made a bold move to open specialty value apparel stores in locations that few others, at that point, had thought to penetrate.

Staking a claim in uncharted territory was the way we planned to expand and diversify our customer base. We believed there was a billion dollars' worth of sales out there that wasn't being monetized.

I was confident we could gain a head start in building a new revenue stream out of specialty value sportswear, accessories, and footwear.

Sell fashion merchandise at sharper pricing: that was the whole point of the value business. Now budget-conscious shoppers had a viable alternative in value strip centers and value malls.

In a specialty-boutique atmosphere, they could shop for trendy clothes that were less expensive and be comfortable among their own peer group. It was a social event that spoke directly to the culture of their generation.

That's why it caught fire. For many customers, a tight budget doesn't go very far when shopping in pricier regional malls. Plus, fashion customers with limited funds would prefer not to always have to shop in a Walmart.

But all that didn't happen overnight. There was a lot of history and previous iterations of the concept that resulted in our creation of the value business while I was at US Shoe Corp.

The two people I trusted most and worked side by side with for decades were *Kim Reynolds*, a supersmart and supertough merchant, and *Perry Bugnar*, a street-smart and hard-driving director of stores. We were a tight-knit unit known within the company as *Bob-Kim-Perry*. That was the nickname given to us by *Ban Hudson*, CEO of US Shoe Corp.

As the 1990s got started, we were in the Washington, DC, market running the *TH Mandy* division of US Shoe Corp. I admit that, with my department store background, I didn't know yet what I was doing in the specialty value retail arena.

## HOW TO DEAL WITH MANDY

Even though *TH Mandy* wasn't very successful, it helped me tremendously. We had the worst real estate, though.

It wasn't always so. *First Lady Rosalynn Carter* shopped there in the 1970s when Jimmy Carter was president of the United States. Two decades later, Mandy stores were shopworn, to put it mildly. But I used that daunting experience as a lesson for the future. I was picking up more *Pieces of the Puzzle* that I would put to good use later in my career.

Ban helped me better understand the ins and outs of marketing. His impressive resume included roles at *Procter & Gamble* and *LensCrafters*.

I agreed with Ban when he suggested we should come up with a new plan for the Mandy stores that we could present to the board of directors of US Shoe Corp. It was either that or shut down Mandy altogether.

Eventually, all but four Mandy stores were closed. Ban and I were eager to rebrand the leftover stores so we could put the Mandy brand behind us and move forward with a new *Vision*.

We both liked the name *Casual Corner & Co.* It capitalized on a strong retail brand, yet at the same time had its own, unique identity.

The president of Casual Corner had other ideas. He was concerned that value-priced stores named Casual Corner & Co. would dilute the unique appeal of his 850-plus Casual Corner stores, costing him sales and revenue.

## VALUE CONCEPT TAKES HOLD

We converted the remaining Mandy stores to what we called *Career Image Company Store*. That allowed us to test the value concept immediately, and customers wouldn't know it actually was Casual Corner merchandise.

Kim, Perry, and I were on our way to Enfield, Connecticut, where Casual Corner was based, to run the new business, and our value concept was on its way to bolstering US Shoe Corp.

However, I still had to contend with my boss, the Casual Corner CEO—and his opposition to our plan to extend his brand to the value segment.

I was presenting to the board of directors of US Shoe my strategy to greatly expand the new value business that I would run for Casual Corner. My new boss felt threatened. He told me outright he wouldn't support me. He was convinced the new value business I was passionate about never would turn a profit.

It was obvious that he resented my expanded responsibilities within the corporate structure. My opportunity to rise through the ranks threatened his own status in the company.

It also was clear that he and I didn't like each other. Our differences came to a head in a heated exchange. Not exactly demonstrating team spirit in the executive suite, the Casual Corner CEO said to me: "I'll be in a prone position before I let your company grow."

I stared straight at him and said, "If you don't believe in me and in growing our business, then you should get ready to be in your prone position."

Nobody was going to get in my way, least of all somebody with a bad attitude. Shortly thereafter, he retired as president of Casual Corner Group.

The person who eventually pushed him aside was more my style. *Michael Searles* had been a top executive at *Toys "R" Us*, one of the country's hottest retail companies at that time, so I knew he could be the real deal.

When he was brought in to run Casual Corner as the new president and CEO, he wanted me to report to someone who was at a level between us. I asked Mike if I could report to him instead. He was pleasant about it, but let me know in no uncertain terms where I stood at that point. Holding his hand at waist level, he said, "You're only this high, Bob."

His point was that I didn't oversee enough stores for him to spend his valuable time working directly with me. Then, he elevated his hand to his own height, saying, "You have to be this high to be able to report to me."

You don't think that moment motivated the heck out of me?

I assured Mike that I'd be able to build the Casual Corner value business without taking up his time. With his direct support of my efforts, I argued, the entire company would benefit and become much more successful in the process.

Within three days, I was back in his office to make my case. I drew him a picture—literally. I showed him a wall chart I had made to illustrate my value store concept.

## THE HOME RUN PITCH

The chart explained the potential for a dramatic payoff in additional revenue if we added value-merchandise stores—branded Casual Corner & Co.—to the existing Casual Corner regular-price business: we could increase our footprint to *2,500* stores, from one thousand, and add *$1 billion* in revenue, for a total of $2.5 billion.

My pitch worked. "Bob, you just went from one foot high to this high," Mike told me, raising his hand level with his head. "You're going to report directly to me, building the value business for Casual Corner Group." That's what I mean by *Putting It on the Line* to get the results you want. I was determined to change his mind, and I did.

After proving the value concept worked in that handful of Career Image stores, the Casual Corner president who was in our way didn't have an argument to hold us back any longer. By the end of 1992, we operated eight stores that had been renamed, or had the new name, Casual Corner & Co.

We focused squarely on operating in outlet centers, where people go to shop for everyday bargains. For Casual Corner, which had not operated stores in those value malls before, we had opened a new frontier—with a major new revenue stream flowing from it. Our new business was beginning to gain *Momentum*, but we still were looked at by the corporate office as a minor part of the overall business.

Then, unexpectedly, someone spoke up on our behalf: *Dave Brown*, who was president and CEO at LensCrafters, a leading division of US Shoe Corp.

Recognizing the potential in our young division, Dave made the point to Ban that just because Casual Corner & Co. still was small compared to more established divisions of the company, it shouldn't be ignored or underestimated. He said we should be supported with significant investment.

## BABY GORILLA

I'll never forget the colorful way he passionately pleaded our case: "Don't starve the baby gorilla," he said. "You need to let him grow."

Dave's message was that the smallest division in the company (the *baby* gorilla) could grow into the biggest division (the *800-pound* gorilla).

The lesson there is that you must be able to recognize when a smaller business segment shows a lot of room for growth; don't make the short-sighted mistake of focusing solely on a larger segment that may be nearing its peak growth. Always look ahead to what could be the next big revenue stream.

After that, Ban started referring to our management trio as "the baby gorilla Bob-Kim-Perry."

As the "baby gorilla," our charge was to create a value business. The day after we changed Career Image Company Store to Casual Corner & Co., sales in those stores shot up 25 percent. Ban couldn't help but notice such a big, immediate bump.

A typical scenario for the dramatic transformation was our Mandy store in Virginia's Potomac Mills mall. Opened in 1986 outside Washington, DC, it was one of the earliest major value centers.

As soon as the Potomac Mills Mandy store was renamed Casual Corner & Co.— with a fresh paint job and new carpet—its gross profit margin increased by more than ten points and its sales increased by 33 percent.

The value-priced merchandise in the refurbished stores had the same feel as Career Image goods, but it was different. Changing the stores' image worked like a charm. With permanent value pricing, we didn't have to cheapen our image by promoting one sale on top of another. Every day was a sale day.

We were the only retailer selling a mix of desirable fashion sportswear brands in an outlet center. We were operating a little blind, learning as we went. This was a new business and we had to make some guesses on inventory levels. Fortunately, that was one of my strengths. Remember, I'm a guy who likes numbers and who likes figuring out how to make them end up in the black.

## THE DESIGNER LABEL SOLUTION

On the plus side, Kim had prepared us well for the new business. She had bought merchandise for the Mandy chain-wide closing sale at steep discounts. That allowed us to mark it up by as much as 70 percent and still offer customers attractive prices.

There was another side, though, that wasn't such a plus: Casual Corner's primary vendors didn't want their labels shown at discount prices in the marketplace. It would conflict not only with Casual Corner's regular-price stores, but also with the vendors' other retailers, which would not like their inventory suddenly being devalued in the marketplace.

That was a major stumbling block for the new stores. We had to find a way around it to keep moving the ball forward.

Then it crossed my mind: What if we created our own Casual Corner & Co. labels? That's the ticket! We ordered the tags from a label maker. The label supplier shipped those labels to the manufacturers of our merchandise. They in turn ripped out their own labels and stitched in our Casual Corner & Co. labels.

Just like that, within a few days, our stores had goods that looked like they were exclusive to Casual Corner & Co. They were the same name brands sold in thousands of other stores, including Casual Corner. That's called private label. That's called creative problem-solving. It was the ideal solution.

All we did was what any smart retailer should do: pay close attention to who the audience is and what they want. Then give them the best of all worlds. A "novel" concept!

I was more eager than ever to shift into higher gear. So was Casual Corner & Co. The eight stores now were ready for the next stage of evolution. Now that we had established a solid base of business in outlet centers, the next step was to extend our footprint into value strip centers and value malls.

# THINK LIKE A BEZOS

Whether you're in charge of a company, a division, or a project team, I believe that the most important thing to remember is this: there is *no secret sauce* for success!

People at the top of their game—such as Amazon founder Jeff Bezos—tell us it is not genius that creates game-changing products and business models. It is good, old-fashioned sweat and the iron will to do **Whatever It Takes** to put your **Vision** into action.

Bezos invested countless hours and years of relentless experimentation and unbridled imagination to create Amazon. The company he built continues to take risks in pursuit of profitable new ideas because Bezos knows that as hard as it is to get to the top, it's even harder to stay there.

"If you only do things where you know the answer in advance," Bezos says, "your company goes away." He adds, "It's the lessons you learn along the way."

"The biggest risk," says Facebook founder Mark Zuckerberg, "is not taking any risk ... [that's] the only strategy that is guaranteed to fail."

## KICKING IT UP IN NASHVILLE

That *baby gorilla* episode with Dave and Ban was a great motivating tool that stayed with me. So much so that when we celebrated our one hundredth store opening of Casual Corner & Co.—in Nashville in 1995—I orchestrated the kind of theatrical stunt that was becoming part of my management style.

The Nashville event was a big deal. The senior management of the parent company, US Shoe Corp., traveled there to congratulate me and our team.

Perry arranged for someone to wear a gorilla costume. At the party, at just the moment when it would have maximum impact, we rolled in a six-foot-tall "package," and, to everyone's shock, out of it burst a life-size gorilla!

I told everyone the story of "not starving the baby gorilla," and exclaimed that we were on our way to becoming a big gorilla.

"You are correct, Bob," Ban said in front of everyone. "You no

The famous baby gorilla memento.

longer are the Bob-Kim-Perry baby gorilla." It was a tribute to how my long-standing team and I were recognized as a strong-performing unit. He then gave me a gorilla with a cowboy hat on it, which I still hold on to as a memento.

I wasn't done reviewing our milestones. In a speech I gave at the Nashville celebration, I shared with everyone something Ban once said to me as I sat in his living room with other US Shoe executives: "Last year," he had said, "you were whale shit scraping the bottom of the ocean floor."

When you are dealing with people who run billion-dollar companies, that's what you have to deal with. You have to know how to respond to that kind of brutal put-down without being defensive. I thought to myself, "I'll show him."

When he told me that, I asked him, "Am I that now?"

He replied, "No, you have now risen to the top."

So, at the Nashville party, I used that crazy anecdote to remind him of that line, and said, "You once told me I was whale shit. Now I am a whale smiling and spouting water on top of the ocean."

Between gorillas and whales, I think I made my point. You can call me whatever you want. I won't be insulted. Being underestimated only makes me fight harder to prove myself, and to make the business succeed for everyone's benefit.

Having grown to 100 stores strong at Casual Corner & Co., our sights now were set on another tier of customers, those who routinely shopped at discounters and off-price outlets. Think **Walmart**, **Target**, **T.J.Maxx**, **Marshall**, and **Kohl's**. To fit in better with that retail environment, we decided another name change was in order. That's how Casual Corner Annex was born.

## PHANTOM MARKET STUDY

As Casual Corner Annex began to take off, Ban asked Mike Searles and me if we had tested the name *Casual Corner Annex* to use it in strip centers and malls. Mike assured him that we had commissioned a study on Casual Corner Annex—but we hadn't.

We never had time to do anything, but we were confident it was the right move. Mike thought the risk in telling the head of the company that we had tested the name was worth it: we wanted to avoid any slowdown in the growth opportunity, and a study would have gotten in our way at that point.

Sometimes it's okay to take a calculated chance like that, but you can only get away with it if you know it's going to be right.

Our attitude was: game on! I was quoted in one of the trade papers as an industry leader, saying, "You're going to see *Casual Corner*, *Old Navy*, and *Ann Taylor* in strip centers now, not just in the malls."

I went from being a little guy at US Shoe, with eight stores, to a big guy—eventually running almost three hundred Casual Corner & Co. stores. I was in the middle of the mix, helping to move the market in a new direction that promised substantial growth in customers, stores, revenue, and profit.

We were on pace to get to one thousand stores when, in 1995, US Shoe was sold to Italian conglomerate *Luxottica*. Its chief executive, Leonardo Del Vecchio, had his own priorities—and Casual Corner & Co. was not one of them. The one thousand-store value-priced business never came to pass at Casual Corner, but *the Best Was Yet to Come*.

With *TH Mandy* and *Casual Corner* as my training ground, I arrived at rue21 with enough *Tribal Knowledge* to build a business based on value malls and strip centers. I was determined to reach the one thousand-store mark, whether it was in Enfield, Connecticut, or in Pittsburgh, Pennsylvania, home of *Pennsylvania Fashions* ... soon to become *rue21*.

# WHEN YOU HIT A DEAD END, BREAK THROUGH THE WALL

Things can be going great, with all signs pointing in the right direction for you and your plans.

Then, without warning, a change in course blows your plans apart and stops you in your tracks.

That's what happened to me when **Casual Corner** was sold. I was moving full speed ahead toward one thousand stores with **Casual Corner Annex**. The new owner had other plans that upended mine. It was a game-changer, but I didn't let it become a game-ender.

I found my way to a different place, where I could use my previous experience productively. The **Pieces of the Puzzle** were coming together.

If you think you are on the road to success, and hit a bump or detour along the way, file away the information you have gathered so you can apply it somewhere else. Those are temporary detours, not dead ends.

The only person who can derail your express train to success is you. Don't forget that!

# CHAPTER NINE

# THE REAL DEALS: LEADERS I HAVE LEARNED FROM

Over my career, a handful of role models inspired me. They taught me valuable lessons. They influenced how I carried out my duties and responsibilities as a manager of businesses—and of people. They inspired me to use some of their best techniques to get the most out of people.

These role models also helped me develop a keen eye and ear for separating *Real Deal* types from (excuse the expression) bullshit executives. There is no shortage of *that* type! They play the game well when it comes to office politics. That's not the same as demonstrating deep *Tribal Knowledge* of a business and its people.

In my experience, the *Real Deal* breed of leaders consists mainly of innovators and influencers who stay within the same industry for their entire career. That speaks to their focus, passion, and wealth of knowledge within a very defined area.

In addition to the people featured in this chapter, three *Real Deal* legends who come to mind are **Leonard and William Lauder** of **Estée Lauder** and *Leslie Wexner* of **L Brands** (**The Limited**, Victoria's Secret, Henri Bendel**, etc.).

Their longevity is as amazing as their business records. As I write this, Wexner has been CEO for more than fifty years, which makes him the longest-serving chief executive of a Fortune 500 company.

The CEOs I don't consider *Real Deal* tend to be executives who jump from one position to another. With some exceptions, they don't stick around long enough to develop a depth of understanding about any one company or its culture.

Instead, they know a little something about each of the different industries they've "visited." Instead of acquiring *Tribal Knowledge*, it's more likely they have picked up trivial knowledge. Rather than innovators or influencers, they are more like caretakers—the proverbial jack of all trades, master of none.

I've known and observed a lot of CEOs through the years, and I have learned valuable lessons from a few of them that I was able to put into practice.

It's said that struggles make you stronger, and I can attest to that. What kind of struggles have you had in your work life so far, and how do you think they have made you stronger? If you tell me that you've had no struggles, I will ask you if you are challenging yourself enough. No pain, no gain.

I never could have learned the business and taken over rue21 without all the experiences and challenges that came before. I learned a lot from other people. I listened. Some were mentors. Some were not.

## ALWAYS BE A STUDENT

What I absorbed from CEOs I have known along the way is of value not only to those in the C-suite. The same lessons can be put into action by managers at any level, and by entrepreneurs.

The worst thing you can be in any walk of life is a know-it-all. It's essential to always be a student. Always pay attention. Always be ready, willing, and able to learn from others. They may be industry icons, as the names in this chapter are. They may be coworkers, bosses, or even family and friends. If you ever have the chance to serve an apprenticeship with someone who is a proven success, grab it. You found a mentor! I'm forever indebted to my mentors for lessons that may have taken me a lot more time to learn on my own, or that I might never have learned.

Strong leaders understand all different types of people. They cannot just connect with others, but also shape their ideas and behavior. There will be some workers who won't let you through, yet it doesn't mean they don't want someone to guide them. The CEO's challenge—one of many to contend with every day—is to size up people quickly.

A good CEO is good at many things. One of those is staying people focused. That's a core skill of leadership.

Leading people effectively and productively has its darker side too. CEOs who perform to their potential, or close to it, do not let distractions throw them off their game. They don't overthink during critical moments in the decision-making process.

It shouldn't be necessary to step on people. What is necessary, when the situation demands, is cutting through nonsense that gets in the way of business and personal advancement.

*Jenny Byrom Betzler* (or Jenny B, as I called her), an assistant buyer working for me, wanted to be promoted to buyer. That's great, but there was a problem: she didn't want her colleagues to think she was trying to get ahead at their expense. "Then you'll never be a buyer," I told her. She listened to me and became an excellent buyer!

It's not about being cruel; it's about training yourself to be immune to certain sensitivities that people naturally will have when you say or do something unpleasant or unpopular. It's inevitable that colleagues compete to advance. It's inevitable that people will try to put you at a disadvantage for their own benefit.

Whether you're in the top spot or not, the criticisms will be mostly behind your back. The best way to defend yourself against the negative remarks is to bear down and do your job as best you can. It's important to be aware of office politics. It's important to position yourself wisely as a hard worker who contributes to the company's success. It's not worth getting bent out of shape about everything said about you, to the point where it distracts you from the job at hand.

During my tenure at US Shoe, I was compared to "whale shit scraping the bottom of the ocean floor." At A&S, I was told I would never amount to more than a merchandise manager. At Casual Corner, I was told I wasn't "high enough" to report to a top executive. None of those slights stopped me. They energized me to succeed.

## LEONARDO DEL VECCHIO

I've been cut down to size by one of the world's richest people, *Leonardo Del Vecchio*, whose face turned red as he said, sarcastically, "I make you emperor!" when I complained to him about my job title.

He was absolutely right in the way he handled it. Together with his son *Claudio*, the Del Vecchios were taking over a very large retail operation for the purpose of making it profitable. Here I was, turning his valuable time and attention away from that to focus on the tiny, unimportant detail of my job title.

Mr. Del Vecchio also happened to be one of the most brilliant businessmen I've work for. He's the head of *Luxottica*, which he founded in 1962. That company name may not be familiar to you, but its brands are world renowned: *LensCrafters*, *Ray-Ban*, *Oakley*, and *Sunglass Hut*.

Mr. Del Vecchio epitomizes what I mean about the occasional need to be *Fearless*. As with any talented CEO, though, that wasn't all that he was about. He also could turn on the continental charm. Most important, as it is for any successful CEO, he had extraordinary strategic *Vision*. In fact, his nickname in Italy is "The Far-Sighted Man." It's not lost on his compatriots that his initials, *LDV,* are the same as another recognizable Italian: Leonardo da Vinci.

He was a fascinating combination of Old World and New World.

The Del Vecchios taught me a lot about the importance of loyalty and trust in business. Another essential quality is integrity. It's important to be able to spot that in others so you are not fooled into following someone who might mislead you.

Working for Mr. Del Vecchio taught me a lot about the workplace culture of Europe, which has many differences from corporate America. Italians refer to bosses like LDV as "my owner." In the same sense, the office you occupy is not really yours. The company is lending it to you, and, at all times, can claim possession of just about anything in it. In the beginning, it was hard to get used to that sensibility.

Maybe the difference in attitude between doing business in Europe and in the US is that European workers can see themselves from management's point of view. They understand that everything has a cost attached to it. Health benefits are not free. Somebody has to pay for them. When you don't assume anything will be given to you, you naturally appreciate it more.

It didn't matter to Mr. Del Vecchio that he was worth billions. He was all about being the complete entrepreneur. He believed any individual running a business—no matter how big it is—has to be visionary and flexible.

I learned from him that you cannot build something through process and procedure alone. What is the *Vision*? What is the goal? Why are you doing it that way?

> **You cannot build something through process and procedure alone.**

I marveled at the loyalty Mr. Del Vecchio had among his workers. They put their trust in him, even though at times they were scared to death about losing their jobs if business didn't improve. They wanted LDV to feel good, as if he were the head of their family. And he was.

It was LDV's influence that led me to insist at rue21 that, even with 1,200 stores, we never referred to a store by number, but by the location and store manager's name.

The culture I created and encouraged at rue21 was the culmination of all my years of experience; learning from others, like LDV; and trusting my own instincts in how to build business and how to make people feel part of a family. Picking up that knowledge bit by bit and putting it together is what I keep referring to as *Pieces of the Puzzle.*

## CLAUDIO DEL VECCHIO

Business brilliance runs in the Del Vecchio family. At Casual Corner, I dealt extensively with LDV's son *Claudio*, who now runs *Brooks Brothers*. In 2002, the younger Del Vecchio bought that legendary brand for the bargain price of $225 million. He has done well restoring Brooks Brothers's prestigious image and value.

Claudio and I are a lot alike in our management philosophy. We both liked to take control. We're both focused first and foremost on the customer. It's always smart business to stay out in front of everybody who is responsible for your success.

Talk to your workers before they talk to you. Know what your bosses expect before they ask you for it. Stay closely connected with the trends your customers are following and the merchandise they're buying.

One of Claudio's first tasks after taking over Brooks Brothers was to read complaint letters from customers. That's the roll-up-your-sleeves, entrepreneurial impulse that both Claudio and I learned from his father.

Not everyone in Claudio's position would be eager to dig deep into piles of letters detailing what's wrong with the company they just bought. That he made it a top priority is what sets him apart as an elite retailing CEO. Claudio also is very good building strong brands. He learned those skills from working at Luxottica with his dad.

Watching, and working with, Claudio, I saw his fierce determination. He wasn't afraid to take risks, to try different things, to move out of his comfort zone when he thought he might discover something new and valuable. Thanks to him, I grew stronger myself in those disciplines. He gave me another important *Piece of the Puzzle* that would help me succeed at rue21.

When I left Casual Corner in November 1999, it was mostly because there wasn't room for Claudio and me to coexist in the same company any longer. We both were strong willed—and his family owned the company.

Claudio was gracious when I departed Casual Corner. He assured me that, no matter where I landed next, I would do well. More than a year after exiting Casual Corner, I started my career at rue21.

After we had become a nationwide, thousand-store retailing phenomenon, whenever I ran into Claudio, it was satisfying to know that what I had built caused him to look at me differently. There was mutual respect, which I value to this day.

Throughout my career, beginning with that first job at A&S, I've been fortunate to know other savvy, successful merchants who have gone on to become legendary influencers in the business world.

## MARK BUTLER

*Mark Butler* of *Ollie's Bargain Outlet* has made it big by making the most of his *Tribal Knowledge.* He's the "real deal," a no-nonsense, results-oriented type of guy.

Mark started Ollie's in 1982. I met him twenty years after that, when both our companies had become part of the same private equity group. Through that connection, I was asked to advise Mark on his growth strategy because of my experience building Casual Corner, whose various divisions added up to 1,500 stores.

When I met Mark, he had fewer than thirty Ollie's stores with revenue of $75 million. By early 2019, the amazing company he built was worth more than $5 billion, with more than 300 stores. Mark and Ollie's were well on the way, as rue21 had been, into becoming one of the leading retail growth stories in the US.

How did Mark Butler do it? *Tribal Knowledge!*

I know firsthand how Mark stands up strongly for what he believes. I've never seen the man back down. When we met in 2003, I was happy to serve as a sounding board to support him and his ambitious plans. All these years later, I feel fortunate to continue advising Ollie's as a member of the board of directors.

He's assembled a loyal corps of hard workers, hiring people he respected, whose support he could count on. The upbeat culture is exemplified by the company chant, "We are Ollie's!" that is heard as a call-and-response during Mark's presentations.

Visit the Ollie's Bargain Outlet website (www.ollies.us) and it's obvious right away that Mark is at the top of his game. Ollie's uses colorful cartoon images to promote popular brands at deeply discounted prices. That playful approach helps him create constant demand through a powerful and unique connection with the customer.

The stores don't try to look fancy. In fact, they are modestly described on Ollie's website as "semi-lovely." That is an effective use of humor to let people know that Ollie's is a casual, no-frills place without pretensions, a place where people will have fun shopping.

In a TV interview, Mark told stock market guru Jim Cramer of CNBC's *Mad Money* that "there's a charm in telling the truth." Sure enough, Ollie's earthy TV commercials exclaim, "Good stuff cheap!" and "The bigger the cheapskate you are, the more you'll save!"

Strategically, Mark and I think a lot alike. We share a tenacity for pushing a business to its upper limits to maximize return on investment. He is my idea of a master merchant. He has an uncanny knack for identifying a business opportunity, and then figuring out the best way to capitalize on it.

Mark's stores do so well because they let customers go on a treasure hunt for good values. That's a great way to drive sales: invite customers on an adventure where they will never know what new bargain they might find.

Figure out what people like and give it to them. Sounds like a simple formula for success. Only a handful of businesspeople, though, know how to scale it for constant, profitable growth.

Mark Butler is one of the few.

## MACON BROCK

Both Mark Butler and I benefited greatly from the mentorship of *Macon Brock*, founder of *Dollar Tree*. I was proud that Macon was a member of my rue21 board.

Dollar Tree, which also owns the **Family Dollar** chain, operates nearly fifteen thousand stores across the US and Canada. As its name plainly says, much merchandise in the stores is priced at a dollar or below.

Macon is another "real deal," filled with *Tribal Knowledge*. He had an unbelievable knack for finding value in unusual, hard-to-find merchandise, traveling with his wife, Joan, to the other side of the world to bring back items that he knew customers would crave. His judgment rarely was not spot on.

With two partners, Macon took an independent toy store business in Norfolk, Virginia, and used it as a foundation to vastly improve on the "dollar store" concept that others had originated in the 1980s. It's a good reminder: when developing a new idea, you don't have to be the first one to market—just the best one.

Dollar Tree employs 165,000 people, is on the Fortune 500, and has annual sales (as of 2019) of more than $20 billion. That business scale is all the more remarkable because it was built, as the title of Macon's autobiography says, *One Buck at a Time*.

Macon taught Butler and me the wisdom of keeping things simple, understanding people, and sticking to the mission. That's a three-pronged philosophy we each put to good use in running our respective retail chains.

Another lesson he taught us is not to overreact to situations. "Just move forward," he would say.

Whenever Macon was at rue21 for a board meeting, he was a magnet for our associates, who flocked to greet him. He enjoyed talking to all kinds of people.

Every life has its chapters, and I have several yet to be written. *Giving Back* is one of those chapters, a work in progress. It's one way to show thanks for the good fortune that has propelled my career, which has a lot of mileage behind it and a lot ahead of it.

Macon could serve as anyone's role model for *Giving Back*. In his hometown of Virginia Beach, Virginia, he funded major endowments at several colleges, as well as supporting environmental advocacy groups and museums.

Macon's remarkable business success has benefited countless people, many of whom have nothing to do with the company he founded. That's because he also was a leading philanthropist whose good works leave a legacy of charity and generosity that we all can learn from, regardless of personal wealth.

Macon Brock, who passed away not long ago, was a great businessman and mentor who will be missed.

## TOMMY HILFIGER

I met Tommy Hilfiger before he was *Tommy Hilfiger*, the famous brand name designer. My sportswear merchant Kim Reynolds and I had dinner with him in 1984 at Joe's Stone Crab, the world-renowned seafood hangout in Miami.

That was the year Tommy was meeting with retailers like *Jordan Marsh*, because we were going to be launching his new sportswear line. His men's line was starting to strengthen, and now he was launching a women's line. He had designed for other companies, like Murjani, which marketed Gloria Vanderbilt jeans. This would be the first time his name was on women's sportswear. He already had come a long way from carrying his samples around on his shoulder.

Not long after we first met, Tommy's name was being mentioned alongside fashion giants Ralph Lauren and Calvin Klein. His appeal, based on cool styling and clever marketing that created a fashion cult, quickly spread beyond a mainly white customer base to a much more diverse base.

Tommy's career is a study in *Tribal Knowledge*.

Like Ralph Lauren and Perry Ellis, he never had formal training in design. Unlike them, Tommy had dyslexia. None of that held him back. He did **Whatever It Takes**. He opened his first store, the People's Place, in his hometown of Elmira, New York, when he was a nineteen-year-old college student.

He also is the model of a **Disruptor** who shook up the fashion business. The aggressively cocky ad campaigns that introduced his brand caused a lot of controversy in the 1980s and earned the then-unknown designer widespread attention. One magazine ran a cover story titled, "Tommy Who-figer?"

During a rough patch that his line faced in the mid-2000s, Tommy became fixated on successful competitors like Abercrombie & Fitch and American Eagle. He wanted to compete with them by copying their fashion style.

But that wasn't him, and it wasn't working. That frustrated Tommy even more. As successful as he had been, Tommy Hilfiger was starting to second-guess himself, moving outside his comfort zone.

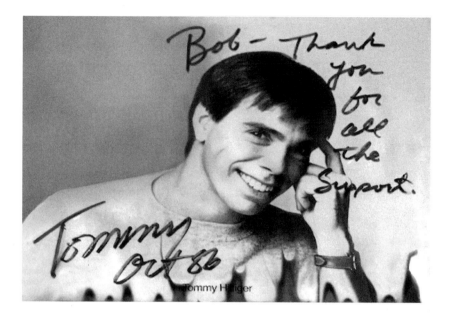

Tommy Hilfiger

At a global CEO conference in 2013, Tommy told the high-level gathering of industry leaders how his company's CEO, *Fred Gehring*, mentored him back to the success that had made him a household name. Fred told him to forget about the competition and to "follow the same instincts that made you successful in the first place."

Tommy took that wise advice to heart. He came back stronger than ever. The Tommy Hilfiger brand was acquired by leading clothing company PVH, whose other prestige brands include Van Heusen, Calvin Klein, Izod, and Geoffrey Beene.

By 2018, Tommy Hilfiger sales had reached $8 billion, quadruple what they had been in the mid-2000s. Now it's an international growth company.

What Tommy Hilfiger was able to do is a great story of resilience and redemption. The lesson is that, while it's smart business to keep track of what others are doing, don't think you should *copy* them. Trust your *Tribal Knowledge* instincts, even when there are obstacles to overcome. Stick to the basics that made you successful in the first place.

Tommy Hilfiger proved beyond a doubt—and probably beyond anyone's expectations—who he is: one of the defining designers of his generation, with impressive crossover appeal to younger generations. That's the true sign of forever fashion, and Tommy is a *Genuine* classic.

## MICKEY DREXLER

When I started at A&S in the mid-1970s, I was immediately drawn to one merchandiser. Although I didn't work for him directly, I saw him as a role model. It was *Mickey Drexler*.

At that time, nobody had heard of better sportswear. The category barely existed. Then along came the ambitious and imaginative Mickey. He made himself a champion of the new category and parlayed it into a legendary retail career.

He had the brilliant idea to put pedigree names like *Pierre Cardin* on sweaters and T-shirts. Nobody had done that before he came along. He nurtured Cardin and other labels into superbrands.

I always looked up to Mickey. He stood out as highly unusual, and that caught my eye. I never wanted to be like everyone else, and Mickey certainly wasn't like everyone else.

What set him apart was his deep understanding that you could expand your total business with a blend of better brands and value brands. He was the ultimate merchant and marketer, with a knack for constant retail reinvention.

Where most talented retail executives are either good businesspeople or good merchants, I could see that this man demonstrated superior *Tribal Knowledge* in both merchandising and marketing.

A&S was regarded in the 1970s as the country's leading department store. There, Mickey and I learned state-of-the-art merchandising and leadership in the trenches. We were taught it's better to confront issues than to fear confrontation. We were in the right place at the right time to learn from the best, and we made the most of it.

When starting out in your career, or further on, the key is to recognize the building blocks you'll want to hold on to for future reference. Those blocks are received wisdom that form the infrastructure for a later opportunity. When the opportunity arises, you'll be ready to hit the ball out of the park!

With the lessons I learned from Mickey and from A&S, I kept adding to that base of knowledge with each successive experience. It's no coincidence that the corporate culture I created at rue21 had echoes of the best practices I picked up at A&S, my first *Piece of the Puzzle*—which also makes it the most precious.

Mickey Drexler hit it out of the park repeatedly, achieving landmark successes at *Ann Taylor*, *Gap*, *Old Navy*, *Banana Republic*, and *J.Crew*. More recently, he created a new, hip clothing brand, *Madewell*, that is part of J.Crew.

That's why Mickey is revered as royalty in our business. His lasting contributions have earned him the admiring title of "Merchant Prince."

## JOE VELEZ

Two years after I started my first job, at A&S, I was a manager. I loved what I was doing. I intended to make it a career. I knew that much after the very first day, which is why I had abruptly dropped my plans to become a marriage counselor once I got a taste of how dynamic retailing could be for a type A personality like mine.

If it wasn't for *Joe Velez*, though, who knows what path I would have taken, and where it would have led. My gut tells me it would not have led to where I am very fortunate, and very happy, to be today.

Managers at A&S in those days earned a salary of $12,000 a year. One day, I received a job offer to be a sales representative at a leading manufacturer. It paid $20,000, a huge 67 percent salary increase. Talk about tempting!

One Friday, I was called to the office of Joe, then an A&S executive vice president. I already had been told he didn't want me to leave. Naturally, I was nervous. Executives at my level normally would not be meeting with someone at his level.

Joe started telling me that he heard I was considering a move. "You will be a buyer here," he said, matter-of-factly, virtually guaranteeing me what was a coveted, powerful position for someone on my career path. A very tiny percentage of those who entered the prestigious A&S executive training program ever made it all the way to full-fledged buyer.

Joe continued the sales pitch meant to keep me from leaving A&S. "If I didn't think highly of you, you wouldn't be sitting here."

Referring to the position I had been offered by the manufacturing company, he continued to press his case for why I should not accept it: "Once a salesman, always a salesman," he said, implying that I would be shortchanging my future career growth. "I think you should learn the skills of being a buyer first before making a change."

It was the biggest decision of my young career. Joe said I should think about his advice over the weekend. He told me to call him on Monday, letting him know if I was staying or leaving.

Without getting up from my chair, I looked at him across the desk, and said, "Mr. Velez, I don't need the weekend. Just the fact you

## THE GRASS RARELY IS GREENER ON THE OTHER SIDE

One of the lessons learned from my Joe Velez encounter is not to let a fat job offer cloud your long-term view. The grass is *not* always greener on the other side. Think hard about whether the opportunity to make a move is the right **Piece of the Puzzle** for you. For me, the better-paying sales job was not the right piece. Joe helped me realize that.

Another critical lesson gleaned from my meeting with Joe, and my decision resulting from that conversation, is that patience *will be rewarded* when you have smart people **Mentoring** you.

There's also such a thing as being promoted too quickly. If you're not ready for the next step, without the necessary experience behind you, the added pressure of an elevated position can cause you to underperform, squandering the valuable job equity you've built to that point. (**Baby Boomers** will recognize that as *the Peter Principle*. Google it.)

would call me to your office like this tells me this is where I want to be. I will show you that I will become a buyer at A&S."

Six months after that life-changing meeting, A&S made me an associate buyer. Six weeks after that, I became a buyer. Joe kept his word, and I kept moving in the direction I wanted.

## MICHAEL JEFFRIES

Like Mickey Drexler, *Michael Jeffries* is another iconic name in apparel retailing who worked at A&S when I started there in the 1970s. He taught me a great deal.

"Mr. Fisch, what is the sales per square foot of this fixture?" he might ask, as I sweated walking the floor of junior sportswear with him. If I said, "I don't know," Michael would then reply, "Maybe you *should* know."

He taught me the finer points of retail merchandising. For example, he would tell me to change fixtures during the day to appeal to an older clientele, and to change them at night for younger customers.

Michael's main claim to fame is reviving and re-creating the **Abercrombie & Fitch** brand. He did it on a scale that nobody could have imagined—and with an inimitable style that is his trademark.

Before Michael came along to transform it, Abercrombie was a famously old-fashioned retailer with a proud but flagging legacy. Founded in the late nineteenth century as a sporting goods specialist, it was out of step with the times. He made it one of the sexiest teen brands of the late twentieth century, appealing specifically to young, hip sophisticates who considered it a status symbol to wear clothing with the Abercrombie logo on it.

Michael also had a knack for attracting controversy, some of which made headlines outside our industry. If I got people talking at the companies I ran, it was because of my hands-on, all-in management style. I've been influenced in that way by very smart people like Michael and Mickey, who became giants of our business.

I still think about A&S as a once-in-a-lifetime training ground. I never forgot what I learned from Michael, Mickey, and Joe. The impression they made on me continues to this day. I hope anyone who has worked for me feels the same way. It's all about leadership.

# CHAPTER TEN

# DO YOU rue? I DO!

## Every incoming caller to rue21 would hear the greeting, *Do You rue? I Do!*

Inside our stores, as well, associates couldn't say it enough. It made customers feel like they were members of a cool club. It was contagious.

"Do You rue? I Do!" Five simple words that mean the world to me. That tagline neatly captures the youthful, trendy spirit of rue21. For more than fifteen years, rue21 *was* my world. A world I created, inhabited, and oversaw.

"Do You rue? I Do!" grew and grew until it came to define our company personality. It didn't hurt that people simply enjoyed saying it. It was like a secret club handshake or our version of a cultural meme.

On occasion, a banker, investor, or analyst who would recognize me in New York City would stop on the street to spontaneously say, "Do You rue? I Do!" I loved hearing that, especially in the least expected places.

To this day, "Do You rue? I Do!" carries unique *Meaning* for me.

It fills me with nostalgia and pride for a time and place of creation, growth, and success. It was a magical experience. I wish everyone can have that same sensation at least once in their life.

"Do You rue? I Do!" proves that the most powerful marketing is organic. There is no purer form of promotion than an impactful saying that people relate to and adopt as their own, through word of mouth. Best of all, that phrase didn't cost us millions of dollars. It was free.

## IN THE BONES: THE BOSS AND ME

Pride and nostalgia were major themes of the award-winning *Springsteen on Broadway* show I saw in 2017. The Boss told some great stories to go along with the songs he performed. I'm not any kind of musician, but there was one amazing story that I instantly could identify with. In fact, what he spoke about energized me.

He said that even as an eight-year-old, he could feel it in his bones that, when he grew up, he would be a famous performer. Of course, today, that's an understatement. He's a living legend who's been at it more than forty-five years, releasing his first album in 1973, the year I started my first job at A&S. He had a *Vision* and knew at a very young age that it would come to fruition.

He fulfilled that *Vision* by doing whatever it took to make it happen. I had the same feelings, though not at that young an age. As a young boy, my mind was on basketball.

When I reached my early twenties, though, I was able to look ahead three, five, eight, or twelve years, and visualize what I would be doing. I just knew it. I felt it. It's not an ego thing. It has more to do with *Vision* and *Confidence*.

## AN AHA MOMENT

As I explained in chapter 1, I didn't initially intend to have a career in retailing. Marriage counseling was my focus: I was enrolled in a master's program at Columbia University.

*Dr. Paul Vahanian*, a marriage counselor, author, and professor at *Columbia*, was my advisor. He was an unusually wise man who taught me an insightful lesson about the role parents play in shaping the psychology of a child.

He instilled in me that children must become their own person. He asked me what I wanted to do with my life. I said that I wasn't positive that I wanted to be a marriage counselor. I had been anxious about fending for myself, wondering if I'd always be dependent on my parents. I assumed, when I was younger, that I would go into my father's manufacturing business in the garment industry. But that type of work didn't appeal to me.

I explained to Dr. Vahanian that my interest in marriage counseling was in part a reaction to seeing my mother and father heading for a divorce. I thought that, by becoming a marriage counselor, I could help them. There was another reason that was more mundane: I had to pick a career and didn't know what else to go with.

# CLIMB YOUR OWN CAREER LADDER

Bruce Springsteen didn't create one of the greatest careers in show business through luck. He figured out while very young what he needed to do. Then he followed his own plan.

I'm also focused on setting goals. I set deadlines and challenge myself to achieve each goal on time. You can build your own ladder of success too. Challenge yourself. If you don't stretch, you'll underachieve.

Everything I did at work, every day, pointed me in the direction of milestones. Planning, purpose, and confidence became my best friends.

Be both ambitious and selective in your career choices. What are your goals? What is your purpose? If you don't know yet, you're not thinking hard enough about it.

Assess your strengths, which skills you need to improve, and what kind of role best suits your temperament. Decide which strategic career steps to take, so you keep moving with intensity in the right direction. As you grow older, you'll gain more clarity about how to focus your time and energy on what matters and how to be more selfish with your time so you don't squander it.

If you haven't already mapped out your personal ladder of goals to live a fulfilling work life and personal life, time's up! Do it now.

Dr. Vahanian asked me what I wanted to do with my life. My answer was totally candid, as always: I told him that I was adventurous, that I wanted to enjoy myself and have an active social life. I wasn't afraid to admit to him that I valued instant gratification.

I also knew what I didn't want: a job that would be generally predictable day to day. I required a lot more stimulation than that. Law or accounting wasn't for me. I always had worried about others, and finally decided it was time to worry about and take care of myself.

Dr. Vahanian sized me up in that moment. He gave me the simplest and best advice of my life: "I don't think you should be a marriage counselor. It's not for you."

His saying that was anything but disappointing; it was music to my ears! I was so relieved that I didn't have to continue my charade of wanting to be a marriage counselor.

Is your current career path what you most want to do with your life, or is it a compromise? If you don't enjoy what you do, why are you doing it? That's a critical question to confront. It's never too late to make a change if it will improve your sense of fulfillment.

What I experienced the first day at A&S was an epiphany for me. I was excited by the enjoyment and **Confidence** it gave me to be in such a dynamic environment. It was the opposite of predictable. The energy was nonstop. I had found something where I had the freedom to be myself. Have you had an epiphany? If not, I hope you find one. It can be life changing.

The first paycheck I received at A&S was like a pass to get out of jail. I didn't need anybody. I knew I could make it on my own from that day forward, for the rest of my life.

It wasn't about the weekly paycheck—all $165 of it. It's about *loving what you do*. My attitude right then and there was, "I am loving what I do now, and the money will follow."

If you love what you do, it's easier to make the *Vision* a reality. You do it because you want to, not because somebody is telling you to do it.

So, let me ask you this: Are *you* doing what *you* really want to do? Are you in touch with your innermost feelings about what makes you happy?

**Are you in touch with your innermost feelings about what makes you happy?**

Being able to combine the victories of your professional life with the gratification of your personal life is a healthy balance that's worth striving for. You need to savor the joy of both for a full and purposeful existence.

Many obstacles stand in the way, including people trying to deter you. That's business. You have to be relentless to get through it all. It worked for me, because I feed off challenges. I was very fortunate to have found something—almost by accident—that fed my ambition.

That's not to say everything worked out exactly to my liking.

## A YEAR ON THE SIDELINES

As I mentioned in chapter 9, I didn't finish my thirteen-year tenure at Casual Corner as I would have liked. By the time I left, I was turning fifty. I believed at the time that *The Best Is Yet to Come*. I'm not just saying that now in retrospect. I was ready to go full speed ahead!

I sat on the sidelines for a year after Casual Corner. Then I saw a couple of opportunities in the Pittsburgh area that intrigued me. The first position wasn't right for me. The second one was a different story. It was called **Pennsylvania Fashions**, and it intrigued me.

I saw that I could dig in and make a significant difference. The private equity firm that owned part of Pennsylvania Fashions— *Saunders, Karp, & Megrue (SKM)*—agreed with me on just about everything I thought the company needed for me to turn it around. I told them I wasn't going in there to come up short, or to let them down.

Knowing that I couldn't finish my career at Casual Corner on my terms only motivated me more to find a place where I could build something on my terms that was different and even bigger. If you have an idea or an ambition that you think is right, don't let it go to waste. There are no boundaries; the sky is the limit.

That was my mindset when I was hired to run Pennsylvania Fashions.

As I prepared to start the new position, which would fill me with good fortune, I can't say for sure that a guardian angel was watching over me. What I can say for sure is that my fascination with destiny, numbers, and nostalgia hit the trifecta! As reported in the book's opening chapter, my first day on my first job, at A&S, was *June 12, 1973*.

What are the odds that more than a quarter-century later, my first day at the place where I would put together all the *Pieces of the Puzzle* I had been working on all those years since was *June 12, 2001*. A coincidence? I don't believe in them. Every move you make influences the outcomes that define your life.

As soon as I walked into the new position at Pennsylvania Fashions, it was clear I was facing a very challenging turnaround situation. The stores specialized in value apparel. There were 255 locations. Half operated under the name *$9.99 Stockroom*, and half were called *rue21*, combining the French word for a street address, *rue*, with the magical age between youth and adulthood, *21*.

In addition to operating stores as $9.99 Stockroom and rue21, Pennsylvania Fashions had another, less official name: "PU Fashions." It was a bad joke, inspired by pessimism among the private equity partners at SKM that the retailer was a losing proposition that might not survive.

When SKM brought me in to turn around "PU Fashions," the retail operation was running an annual loss of more than $16 million. I wasn't surprised. There was no clear *Vision*, no viable strategy for success.

## RED FLAGS IN THE FIELD

The support center had a modest staff of seventy-two associates. We were in a 13,000-square-foot space rented from a pet supply company that used the rest of the building as its distribution center. The pungent odor of pet food would waft over to where we ate lunch. Not exactly prestigious surroundings.

Meanwhile, out in the field, I observed some red flags about the less-than-professional company culture.

One of those flags was at a store in Las Vegas, where I saw a clerk walking around in bare feet. During my conversation with her, she told me that cash routinely was taken from the register to pay the store's utility bills.

I made a note to myself: "This is a mom-and-pop operation. Too much tolerance of mediocrity and they don't know how to raise the bar higher to get to the next level."

The writing on the wall was as big and bright as the neon signs of the Vegas strip: I had my work cut out for me. First, I had to keep this sinking ship afloat, and second, I had to turn the ship around.

Building a brand, hiring the best people, choosing the right merchandise at the right prices, creating a fast-paced fashion shopping experience, and opening stores: all that was part of the formidable challenge I faced.

I brought on board two people I had relied on and trusted implicitly at Casual Corner: head merchant Kim Reynolds and director of stores Perry Bugnar. They were my foundation. I would build around them an "A-Team" of experienced, innovative retailing professionals. I needed people like them whom I could count on, and who knew how I thought and worked.

At the time I came on board, $9.99 Stockroom was a conservative, preppy-style teen apparel retailer, selling khakis, cargo shorts, and flannel shirts at $14.99 and less. I thought it was a great recipe … for going out of business. Everything about it was dated. There was no *newness*.

Looking at the retail landscape at the time, I saw that when companies like ***American Outpost, Clothestime, Accessory Place***, and others went out of business, nobody filled the void.

Those stores closing down didn't mean there wasn't demand by millions of customers in hundreds of towns that were now underserved. The set of circumstances created a perfect opportunity for the emergence of the value retail business.

The rue21 business model was staring me in the face. I was determined to take advantage of it, and to get out in front of the new trend in retailing.

My growth plan was to go more aggressively after the teen market and to become stronger in accessories. We would extend our reach into strip centers and value malls, just as I had started to do at Casual Corner & Co.

# "HIT 'EM WHERE THEY AIN'T"

There once was a New York Yankees major league baseball player who explained his success at the plate with the quirky remark that he "hit 'em where they ain't."

What he meant is that the way for a batter to reach base safely is to hit the ball anywhere in the field except where there is someone in a position to catch it for the out.

It's the same for success in business. If there's a market crowded with competition and another market without a lot of competition but enough customers looking for more places to shop, it's not hard to figure which market is worth cultivating.

At rue21, our unique success came from pursuing the value segment of specialty apparel retailing in strip and outlet centers and value malls. While other retailers remained starry eyed, dazzled by fancy lifestyle malls, we saw greater opportunity closer to earth.

Like that ballplayer, rue21 "hit 'em where they ain't" by taking advantage of smaller, lower-income markets where teens were thrilled to shop in a cool environment for value-priced, fashionable merchandise that was hard to find closer than fifty miles outside their towns.

I used the country's largest retailer as a compass for selecting new sites. Walmart was a magnet for shoppers, but it wasn't exactly considered fashion forward. That's where rue21 came in. We would become the go-to value fashion specialty store in the markets we entered.

## THE AGELESS AGE

One of my first decisions to move in that direction was to change the name of all $9.99 Stockroom stores to rue21. My rationale was that this is the "Age of Aspiration." Teenagers can't wait to be twenty-one. People in their twenties and thirties associate twenty-one with a youthful state of mind more than an age.

Before we could launch into my big plan to create a specialty apparel value retailer with more than one thousand stores, there was

something we needed to do first: file for voluntary bankruptcy.

We entered Chapter 11 in February 2002, giving us cover to continue operating and regain our footing. The court-authorized protection that Chapter 11 of the bankruptcy code makes possible would allow us to generate cash flow without falling behind on payments to vendors and others. The businesses to whom we owed money agreed to cooperate to keep us going.

One of the bank advisors working with us sounded more like he was working against us. He said he anticipated we'd eventually go into what he called, sarcastically, "Chapter 22." If we came out of Chapter 11, he predicted, we eventually would end up having to file for a second Chapter 11. Two of those, he reasoned, equaled "Chapter 22."

Hearing what he said made me that much more committed to building a successful new business that defied doubters like him.

I don't let that nonsense get under my skin. It's just more fuel for the fire that keeps me going. Being vindictive in return saps your energy and gets you nowhere. I had the last laugh anyhow, because his "Chapter 22" prediction couldn't have been more wrong.

Our experience in bankruptcy was an object lesson about how easily misunderstood Chapter 11 can be. Under the right circumstances, it can be a godsend. It was for us. When used properly, Chapter 11 is a smart business strategy for a company that needs to buy time so it can turn around its fortunes and become profitable again. The moment we filed for bankruptcy was the moment rue21's future became brighter. More than that, we were on our way to making retail history.

rue21 went on to record eleven straight years, or forty-five straight quarters, of achieving our sales and profit plan as a high-growth company. That kind of streak is a rarity in retailing. It is one of my proudest milestones.

While we were in bankruptcy, odd as it sounds, I enjoyed the experience. It taught me a lot. When you are doing well while operating in bankruptcy, you are always in control. I knew we could fix what was wrong with the company.

During the year of bankruptcy, we went from the prior year's loss of almost $17 million to a profit of more than $3 million, for a net gain in sales of approximately $20 million. The positive cash flow enabled us to pay back factors who had extended us credit. It allowed us to give bonuses to our associates. The strategy of bankruptcy as salvation had worked.

## EMERGING FROM BANKRUPTCY

We were in Chapter 11 only one year before reemerging stronger, more streamlined, and more confident than we had been. While in bankruptcy, we got rid of bad inventory and closed eighty-five stores, leaving us with 170.

I kept open selected locations that were losing money because my gut said they would return to profitability—and they did. At the support center, we streamlined administrative processes and closed an office that we didn't need.

The new rue21 was a much different story from "PU Fashions." The red ink that stained both the spreadsheet of Pennsylvania Fashions and the portfolio of SKM now was flowing black, with double-digit, year-over-year sales gains.

After we brought the retailer out of bankruptcy, and its performance chart climbed steadily upward, in the eyes of our now-happy equity partner SKM, the company zoomed from zero to hero.

In addition to renaming all the locations rue21, we rebuilt each store from the inside out: new architecture, new layout designs, and new merchandising. For some locations in value strip outlet centers, we added parapets to the exterior facade to give the stores a larger, stand-alone appearance.

Numerous other changes were made to entirely metamorphose the business. What had been an industrial-looking mall retailer in the Midwest and Northern US was becoming one of the fastest-growing specialty apparel retailers throughout the nation.

Still, I had to deal with the usual back-seat drivers. Whenever you're reinventing a business, especially a specialty retailer, plenty of doubters will question your general strategy and your specific tactics.

"Why aren't you more like American Eagle, Abercrombie, and Aéropostale, Bob?" That was a question I heard more than once about the so-called "three A's." I hated hearing it. One answer is because there was a niche in the market waiting to be filled. None of those glitzy "A-list" chains were filling the gap (excuse the pun). None of them would be caught dead in the kind of value strip center where we thrived. You can bet I wasn't complaining about that.

There's another reason I wasn't interested in mimicking the three A's: throughout my retail career, it was never my style to follow the crowd. Being bold and unorthodox is where I found the most success and gratification.

The strength of the rue21 brand was obvious whenever my senior team and I traveled to a state to visit our stores. As often as not, we'd be greeted by rue21 store associates and customers who told us they loved the brand. They saw it as an influential, distinctive part of their lifestyle.

## PEOPLE BEFORE DATA

I've never believed in relying too heavily on analytical data to make merchandising and marketing decisions. What comes first, always, are people, along with gut instincts for selecting merchandise that customers love. That cannot be emphasized enough. Crunching numbers to detect trends using cutting-edge technology is important, but it's no substitute for the human factor: exercising your sensibility as a merchant is what makes or breaks your bottom line.

Putting in place the right people sets you up nicely for the next ingredient of success: *Building a Culture*. There are two cultures to consider: the company culture and the customers' store experience.

If done right, a corporate culture catches hold from the corner office. It can't be dictated or legislated. It has to be felt by just about everyone throughout the organization. It has to be sincere.

People can detect a prima donna CEO whose style is "Do as I say, not as I do." I am the opposite. My attitude is to be as I want everyone else around me to be: hardworking, enthusiastic, fun-loving, helpful to others, team players. I did my best to create a constantly upbeat, uplifting **Culture**.

If you watched a highlights reel of rue21 through the years, you'd see a lot of happy people enjoying themselves. That was especially true at the colorful, high-energy annual events we put on for district managers. One year, the theme was Woodstock's fortieth anniversary. Another time we had an Alter Ego party. Another popular theme everyone loved was dressing in the high society style of the Great Gatsby era.

But happy people also could be seen on any regular workday at their desks, at meetings, and at planning sessions. I wouldn't have it any other way. We developed a great relationship understanding each other while building rue21.

"It's having fun," as one division manager described it. "It's dealing with fashion; it's having that energy level."

At one point, I placed around the office boxes that invited people to "express wildies." I learned that phrase when I sat on the board of *Children's Place*. Fellow board member *Malcolm Elvey* told me the term wildies was South African slang for doing something outrageous outside your comfort zone. I encouraged everyone at rue21 to think out of the box by putting their ideas in a box.

The Alter Ego party was a radical way we pushed people to test the limits of their comfort zones. Sure, it was a lot of fun and everyone enjoyed it greatly. The real point of it, though, was to help everyone stretch their imagination and their self-confidence in a way that also would benefit their work performance. You'd be surprised what you can find out about your own potential when you look at yourself differently.

My alter ego at the party was a current rock star, so I decided to be like *Adam Levine* of Maroon 5. As with everything else, I didn't want to do it halfway, so I lost about fifteen pounds to fit into tight jeans and a torso-hugging tank top, and had tattoos professionally painted on both arms for the event.

The Alter Ego party was the best event rue21 ever threw for its associates. It moved people out of their comfort zones to be what they envisioned in their inner being. We wanted people to strut their stuff with *Confidence*. From all indications, it worked as intended.

This is a great exercise to try on for size yourself: to match your outer being with your inner being. You no doubt have an alter ego in mind, if not more than one. A celebrity, perhaps, or even someone you know whom you admire and would like to emulate. Did you ever think about actually dressing and even acting like that person just to stretch your imagination and expand your confidence?

Understandably, you might feel too self-conscious to do it in public, say at a restaurant. But you can get some friends together and have your own alter ego party in someone's home to keep it private. I encourage you to give it a try! Taking a risk like that is liberating. You never know—you may start doing it on a regular basis!

Our company mantra of "Do You rue? I Do!" created an emotional connection. Asking "What does it mean?" is a fair question. The answer is that it's not about the *Meaning*. It's about what the person saying it feels: "I like shopping here." "I like working here." Even, for investors, "I like owning shares here."

No one ever thought that rue would succeed. It not only succeeded; it grew into the largest-ever specialty apparel retailer by store count in the US. rue21 became a fast-paced teen fashion business throughout all forty-eight continental states, with strength in strip centers, malls, and outlet centers.

## VISION IS VITAL

When stepping into the top spot at a company, I see my role as getting people to adapt to a new environment. If you have a **Vision** to build something, it won't happen unless you can get people to go along to see and execute your **Vision**. If it sounds simple, it's anything but. It takes constant pushing and motivating people who want to be challenged and led. People want to feel they belong. You need to create a culture that supports your business **Vision**.

This is something you should be thinking about. Do you want to move in that direction?

Our ultimate market model was what I mentioned earlier: **The New Retail Reality**. We focused on flexible, fast-paced fashion, aimed at teens and people in their twenties and thirties. The common theme was wanting to capture the ageless vibe of being twenty-one. That gave us a wide base of customers.

Only three years after our Chapter 11, business was so good we tripled the size of our support center to 90,000 square feet to accommodate up to four hundred associates (up from the seventy-two I started with in 2001). A few years later, our distribution center doubled in size to 370,000 square feet.

By fall 2009, the rue21 concept was in full swing. We had opened more than 500 stores in forty-three states, finding our groove in small to midsize markets with populations of 25,000 to 200,000.

Why did it work so well? At every point in my career, no matter where I was employed, I always followed the mantra to "think like the customer." I always believed you cannot go wrong sticking to that mindset.

## HIGH-SPEED FASHION

We knew our target audience wanted to stay on the cutting edge of fashion trends—to be fashion forward. That meant we had to know which designs were hot and then get them into our stores as soon as possible. We would monitor fashion magazines to see what influential celebrities were wearing. We created a strong speed-to-market approach. From order to delivery, fashion items could be on our shelves within seven days to eight weeks.

When *Michael Jackson*'s death shocked the world in June 2009, within six days, in reaction to consumer demand, we had Michael Jackson T-shirts in all our stores. As quickly as the demand spiked, it subsided, and we just as quickly got out of that specialty item. That's as good an example as any of how nimble and flexible we were in meeting instant demand for a one-off product and not getting stuck with excess inventory.

There was no bigger hit in our stores than the themed dressing rooms. With Top 40 music blaring, young customers could go in as themselves and walk out of the room as a rock star, a princess, a club partygoer, or a Hollywood celebrity.

On average, our customers would shop in a store one to three times a week. And we never stopped coming up with new reasons for them to make repeat trips.

In 2006, we rolled out a major new division under the banner of "etc!" It was the industry's first specialty retail accessory business within a sportswear environment. After successfully testing etc! in six of our stores, it exploded into all of our locations.

What had been a marginal business, contributing only 5 percent to overall sales, soon expanded into a $300 million category, accounting for more than a quarter of all rue21 sales.

Included in the etc! departments were exclusive lines of more than twenty fragrances, lingerie, footwear, handbags, and jewelry. Our footwear business grew into the third largest among US specialty apparel retailers. In fact, customers started shopping at rue21 because of our footwear department, and then would also make sportswear purchases.

By 2009, six years after emerging from Chapter 11, we had more than 500 stores. rue21 was the number-one apparel specialty retailer in the country in growth and comparable store increases (for stores opened more than a year).

Especially gratifying is how our success was used as a classic case study in a standard-reference textbook considered an industry bible for college students—*Retailing*, published by the National Retail Federation.

On page 12, accompanying a profile of rue21, is a photo of me straightening a display in a store. The caption said that rue 21 "has a very hands-on CEO." The profile reported that "rue21 has propelled itself forward in the fashion industry during a time when many others are struggling to remain profitable."

All the pieces were falling into place very nicely for rue21 to take the next big step that would cement its market dominance as a value specialty apparel power retailer: an initial public offering.

## MEET SADIE ROBERTSON

We had our ups and downs, but I never doubted that we would build the retail juggernaut that we did, because of the great people around me. My conviction in our ability to overcome obstacles underscores the essential ingredient of success known as *Confidence*.

The definition of that word is simple: believe in yourself. There are only two people who can get in the way of your success: you, and anybody whom you let get in your way. Other than that, it's an open field for you to take the ball and run it into the end zone.

**There are only two people who can get in the way of your success: you, and anybody whom you let get in your way.**

Take *Sadie Robertson*, for example. In 2014, I saw this remarkable teenager on the TV show *Dancing with the Stars*. She is from the family who starred on the reality TV series *Duck Dynasty*. Her grandfather Phil Robertson had created the hugely successful Duck Commander bird-call device.

Sadie captured the imagination of millions watching Season 19 of *Dancing with the Stars*, including my wife, **Stephanie,** and me. Overnight, she became like a new "America's sweetheart." Sadie never had danced before, yet she was so determined and had prepared so diligently, she nearly danced away with the trophy, scoring nines and tens and finishing a strong second in the competition. It was obvious

From left to right: Stephanie Fisch, me, and Sadie Robertson.

to me that here was a *Fearless* young woman going after her dream without hesitation and with pure joy.

As I learned more about Sadie, despite our decades of difference in age, I could see we were kindred spirits. When a *Millennial* and a *Baby Boomer* see things the same way, you have two *Millennial Baby Boomers*! Both of us enjoy motivational speaking as a way to give back to others. She exudes *Genuine* passion on talking tours when she speaks to her peers about faith, urging them to take charge of their lives. She reminds me of me: I get all pumped up when talking to young people about putting it on the line by taking risks and trusting their instincts.

I have some catching up to do with Sadie on the book front, though. This is my first effort, while she has authored two titles, *Live Original* and *Live Fearless*. She also has several business ventures … and the list goes on. She has boundless energy and enthusiasm for all that she does.

That's why Sadie, while still a teen, became a hugely popular role model for her generation of Millennials, including rue21 customers and our associates.

It was that realization—combined with my *Confidence* that anything is possible—that prompted me to tell my senior staff in 2014 that we should recruit Sadie Robertson as a rue21 spokesperson. They looked at me funny, but I was totally serious.

It turned out that my *Confidence* was well placed. Sadie visited our offices and came to our district manager meetings. On the way to a rue21 district manager party, I was beaming as I sat with her in a vintage 1968 Oldsmobile Delta convertible.

At the event, I found myself dancing with a finalist from *Dancing with the Stars*. How did I go from watching her at home on a TV show to dancing and working with her as a rue21 spokesperson with her own clothing line (which we sold)? *Vision* and *Confidence*. Today, I count Sadie Robertson as a good friend.

# CHAPTER ELEVEN

# GOING PUBLIC, GOING PRIVATE

## "Perhaps it's no wonder that more teens are saying good-bye, Abercrombie & Fitch, and hello, rue21."

That was the opening observation of an article in the May 2009 issue of *Retailing Today*. The timing of that piece was right on the money. It couldn't have been more bullish if we had written it ourselves.

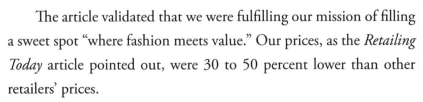

PIECE OF THE PUZZLE

IPO
11.13.09

The article validated that we were fulfilling our mission of filling a sweet spot "where fashion meets value." Our prices, as the *Retailing Today* article pointed out, were 30 to 50 percent lower than other retailers' prices.

rue21 was preparing to go public later in the year. Everything that upbeat article said was a testament to why we were ready to share the wealth in the marketplace with an initial public offering (IPO).

*Retailing Today* was describing **The New Retail Reality** (as I called it), and how that dramatic market development positioned rue21 to continue the growth and profitability we were experiencing, even as other apparel retailers were experiencing hard times.

One retail analyst told the publication, "What America's looking for is more inexpensive, trendy places. Our fascination with Abercrombie and Bebe and Benetton—it's over. Clearly, they are overpriced."

After all, there was a recession going on. To be reeling from its damaging effects was normal for the retail business—or just about any business sector.

In sharp contrast, the vibrant growth of rue21—amid the economic tailspin that bloodied businesses starting in 2008—was anything *but* normal.

*Retailing Today* reported that more than half of teens, in a survey by a firm called WSL Strategic Retail, said that they "now think about whether their parents will be able to afford something before they buy it, and 45 percent said they have to buy more things using their own money."

The publication went on to say that "rue21 proves that trading down can still mean trendy."

As the article reported, rue21 was offering girls and guys "all the latest looks—minus the sticker shock of [our] competitors." Everything in the store was seen as a great value.

# Positioning rue21 for a Premium Valuation
## Strong Growth & Momentum

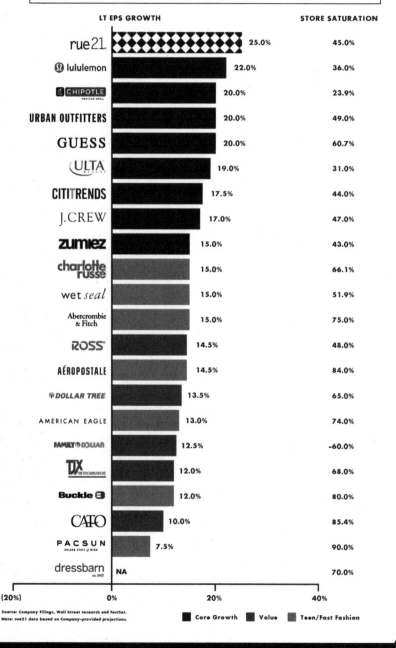

### SUPERIOR GROWTH POTENTIAL

| | LT EPS GROWTH | STORE SATURATION |
|---|---|---|
| rue21 | 25.0% | 45.0% |
| lululemon | 22.0% | 36.0% |
| CHIPOTLE MEXICAN GRILL | 20.0% | 23.9% |
| URBAN OUTFITTERS | 20.0% | 49.0% |
| GUESS | 20.0% | 60.7% |
| ULTA BEAUTY | 19.0% | 31.0% |
| CITITRENDS | 17.5% | 44.0% |
| J.CREW | 17.0% | 47.0% |
| zumiez | 15.0% | 43.0% |
| charlotte russe | 15.0% | 66.1% |
| wet seal | 15.0% | 51.9% |
| Abercrombie & Fitch | 15.0% | 75.0% |
| ROSS | 14.5% | 48.0% |
| AÉROPOSTALE | 14.5% | 84.0% |
| DOLLAR TREE | 13.5% | 65.0% |
| AMERICAN EAGLE | 13.0% | 74.0% |
| FAMILY DOLLAR | 12.5% | -60.0% |
| TJX THE TJX COMPANIES INC | 12.0% | 68.0% |
| Buckle | 12.0% | 80.0% |
| CATO | 10.0% | 85.4% |
| PACSUN GOLDEN STATE of MIND | 7.5% | 90.0% |
| dressbarn est.1962 | NA | 70.0% |

(20%)   0%   20%   40%

Source: Company Filings, Wall Street research and FactSet.
Note: rue21 data based on Company-provided projections.

■ Core Growth  ■ Value  ■ Teen/Fast Fashion

## 1000 STORES OR BUST!

From 2005–2009, rue21 doubled its size in total sales and store count. We were poised to repeat that pace between 2009 and 2014, becoming a one thousand-plus-store company. The fact that we did what we said we would do was, in itself, a formidable achievement. Talk is cheap; results are all that matter.

It's not just that rue21 was making things happen that drew the attention of the rest of the retailing world. We were doing it on the heels of the worst recession in decades. That seemed to defy logic, which only made our story that much more compelling—and impossible to ignore. A lot of eyes now were on us.

Retail industry leaders and Wall Street market makers began to wonder, "What will rue21 do next?"

It was the summer of 2009, and we had the answer: *We are going public!*

There are valuable lessons that come out of the rarefied air that surrounds a company about to sell shares to let the public participate in its growth. I think of the lessons in this chapter as **Fisch Tales Fundamentals for Success** (plus, see the **Fundamentals** at the end of the book).

**Connecting with the Customer** is, of course, a retail necessity, and it's an area where rue21 excelled. At the store level, **The New Retail Reality** had a stronger **Customer** focus. We jumped on top of trends immediately and got out of them as fast as they faded.

We were **Listening** to the market and responding to it by building the right **Culture**. People loved shopping in our stores. They'd come in one to three times a week, including moms with daughters (both would make purchases). The "everybody wants to be twenty-one" culture we cultivated worked like a charm.

When you walked into a rue21, you'd immediately see and feel our distinct and colorful *Culture.*

We turned an otherwise plain fitting room into a make-believe world to help our customers feel special for a couple of minutes. We played Top 40 music that store associates sang as they worked, which encouraged customers to join in. It created a cool atmosphere shoppers wanted to stay in.

The store environment sold itself, as did the personalities and demographics of the store staff, which mirrored the customer base. It was a model of organic marketing.

Growth for rue21 came not just from new store openings but also from converting existing stores to add square footage, for the sake of *Diversification.*

Diversification and the extension of product lines are critical to any growth strategy. Our diverse assortments were about building brands to drive traffic and loyalty. They create a comfort level for the customer that brings people back to the store. They adopt it as their personal brand because of the exclusivity: they can't buy it anywhere else.

In 2006, accessories were emerging as part of *The New Retail Reality.* We created etc! to take advantage of demand for accessories.

Adding etc! changed the footprint of our stores—which became 25 percent larger—and enhanced the rue21 image, broadening our appeal to future stockholders.

After etc!, rue21 was like a reborn company. Other retail apparel stores didn't have the strong accessories franchise that we had built from the ground up. Adding that merchandise was integral to the rue21 growth strategy, and further paved the way to our coming-out party as a public company.

## SWEET SMELL OF SUCCESS

Fragrances became a great add-on business for rue21.

Within a short period, what started as zero fragrances soon grew into twenty. We became the dominant retailer for that category in the value retail sector. My wife, Stephanie, was in charge of our fragrance business. Thanks to her knack for understanding what the customer wants, and her talent for building a brand, fragrances grew into a $50 million revenue stream for rue21.

The new revenue stream wasn't just a success story for our top line. rue21 fragrances threw off high profit margins and became a significant part of our product mix. You even could say they disrupted our business, but in the best way possible. Fragrances became central to rue21's brand, more so than sportswear was. We were changing the perception of rue21, while broadening our appeal.

*Pink Ice*, in particular, was a runaway hit. We sold one million bottles in one year, making it the second-largest selling fragrance (in units) in the US. That single, tiny pink bottle was a giant changemaker, contributing 1 percent of rue21's annual revenues. That's huge.

rue21's fragrance category was created because it was the right move at the right time. It flourished because Stephanie listened to the customer. The numbers proved that she was the best person to run that business, regardless of her husband being the CEO. My belief in her abilities was further vindicated when rue21 in recent years brought back its fragrance division, building on the foundation Stephanie had created.

rue21's fragrance franchise during our tenure grew to 5 percent of total company sales. It also became a big part of our efforts to build exclusive brands. Turning conventional retail wisdom on its head, instead of naming fragrances after sportswear lines, we built out the rue21 master brands by creating sportswear subbrands that were named for our fragrances.

## WHAT'S YOUR VISION?

*The New Retail Reality* was a *Vision* I believed in with total *Confidence*. My *Vision* happened to focus on a retailing concept known as *Speed to Market*.

For rue21, *Speed to Market* meant always having fresh merchandise on display that both reflected and influenced customer tastes, adding 100 stores a year, building each store within six weeks, and recouping investment in a new store in a year or less.

*Speed to Market* became a singular strength for rue21 that no other retailer in our category executed better.

The details of my—or any—*Vision*, though, are not the point here. The starting point is asking yourself if you have a *Vision*. Don't assume that the importance of *Vision* applies only to someone who sits atop a company. No matter what you do for a living or what position you hold, you should be asking yourself, "What's my *personal Vision*?"

It may be your concept of a specific project you're working on, or an ambitious business plan. The more ambitious the *Vision*, the better. The more you need to stretch to see it through, the better it will serve you in the future.

> **A *Vision* is as real as you want to make it, and as unreal as you don't want to make it.**

One word to get out of your head when dreaming up a *Vision* is "unrealistic." A *Vision* is as real as you want to make it, and as unreal as you don't want to make it.

If anything, whether your *Vision* is about a commodity or a service, it is important for it, in some way, to be different from what's already on the market. That could mean better quality, better value, a better solution, supplying unfulfilled demand, or—perhaps the greatest marketing achievement of all—creating demand where none existed. All are examples of *Vision*. I'm sure you can come up with more of your own.

Also important, whether you're in a leadership position or otherwise, is *Alignment* of the *Vision* among all stakeholders.

## THE SECRET SAUCE OF SUCCESS

No matter how clear and compelling your *Vision* may be to you, one or two people can throw it off course by not buying into it as a viable idea. Even worse is having people in your organization trash talk about the *Vision* to others.

It is people who are the secret sauce of success. You have a business to build. You need the right product or service that consumers want. But, more than anything, to get there, you need the right people to be *Aligned* with your *Vision*.

During the road show for our initial public offering, rue21 chief financial officer *Keith McDonough* followed my presentation by running down the numbers. He would begin by saying, "This business is completely *Aligned* under Bob's *Vision*. Everywhere you look, you can see the management team *Alignment*, you can see the organizational *Alignment*, you can see the strategy *Alignment*."

The same was true of our equity partner and majority owner, *Apax*, which also demonstrated total *Trust* in what we were doing by not selling a single share of its rue21 stock. Apax's confidence that our stock's value would continue to rise was a powerful statement of

Do you rue? I do!

The back cover of the rue21 IPO prospectus,
featuring my rue teammates.

total belief in the strength and future of the company.

Nowhere is my regard for loudly recognizing the efforts of people more obvious than the back cover of the prospectus of our initial public offering. The typical IPO prospectus is intentionally dry. It's a financial document, after all, not a lifestyle magazine. But, as is *my* style, I wanted our prospectus to be noticeably different from every other prospectus.

Normally no one would think to put photos of associates (at every level, not only executives) on the back cover of a prospectus—so that's exactly what we did. I was fully aware it might appear corny to some conservative types. So what? I didn't care about that kind of reaction. I was making a statement that "these are the people lifting us up to success." It is important to show the many faces that make that success possible.

# CAPTURING CONFIDENCE

Every salesperson knows that the key to closing the deal is overcoming objections by the buyer. It's the same deal with **Confidence**. You need to overcome doubts to sell yourself ... *to you*!

**Confidence** comes from two places: your head and your heart. Sometimes they don't see eye to eye. That *steals* your **Confidence.** Instead, you want to *steel* your **Confidence**.

In your heart, you may feel a strong passion that you have what it takes to get the job done. Your **Confidence** fills you up with energy.

Then, after a couple of missteps or disappointments, your head starts playing tricks on you. You begin to doubt yourself. Stop! **Trust** the **Confidence** you started with. It's not your imagination. It is real. Let it happen.

**Confidence** means focusing on what is important and ignoring unimportant nonsense that doesn't move you closer to your goal.

**Confidence** means not letting the criticisms or doubts of others undermine your strength of purpose. You can't please everybody, so don't try to, but you absolutely must please yourself.

We are capable of whatever we set our minds to accomplishing. Car pioneer Henry Ford put it this way: "Whether you think you can, or you think you can't—you're right."

Our high-growth, fast-fashion appeal was the kind of opportunity investors look for in a public offering. They're also investing and trusting in a proven management team. We boasted a brain trust of veteran merchants. Six of our seven senior executives, including myself, had been in retailing for at least twenty-five years each.

Our track record for opening stores quickly, cheaply, and profitably (paying back investment in less than a year) played exceedingly well to a market that was hungry for rapid growth and fat margins.

There was more good news for investors sizing us up as a potential darling of Wall Street whose stock value would steadily increase: we were in the process of more than doubling the size of our distribution center to support more than 1,300 stores. We also had limited competition in our retail locations.

Going public was the most amazing experience in my life. It's hard to describe the feeling of seeing all these people wanting to buy into rue21 because they heard it was the hottest retailer in the industry.

## WALL STREET BANKERS "FLIP" FOR rue21

I knew that I had convincingly conveyed the spirit of our rue *Culture* when we were meeting with bankers who wanted to underwrite our IPO. I'm talking about the buttoned-down suits at *Goldman Sachs, Bank of America, and JP Morgan*. They all wanted to underwrite our initial public offering.

They'd come in their standard-issue Wall Street uniforms of dark, pinstripe suits and there we were in our jeans. It was a full-on culture clash, and I wasn't about to have any of it.

I told Goldman Sachs representatives that if I saw a tie at the next meeting, I would cut if off. They got the message. At the next meeting, although they came in again with their ties and suits, instead of shoes they wore flip-flops.

I had the same conversation with Bank of America's people. Their response to what I said was very creative—and very effective. The pitch book they assembled to win our business featured their college photos, so they were pictured as the same age as our target audience. The result was not only playful but proved they could relate to who we were and who our customers were. I of course loved it! They were on board with the rue21 *Culture*.

Being smart about how you do business is not always just about business. It's about relating to the people with whom you are doing business. The bankers were moving out of their comfort zone to form a bond with us. They *Put It on the Line* to impress on rue21 that they would do right by our *Vision* in helping to execute our IPO *Strategy*. The message got through: we were rue21, the age everyone wants to be—including no-nonsense bankers.

When I look back on it now, I almost have to laugh at the crazy logistics you have to survive when pitching your company to investors in an IPO.

We had sixty-five appointments in eight days. Eight of the appointments took place in just one day, in three cities spread clear across the country. At the end of each day, I would sit on the phone with the bank to decide how many shares we potentially had sold so far (people had pledged to buy them but had not yet paid for nor received them).

## $2 BILLION OVERSOLD

The response was overwhelmingly enthusiastic. By day two of the road show, we were ready to sell out the number of shares we wanted to distribute. The demand for the shares more than equaled the supply.

Ringing the opening bell at the Nasdaq MarketSite on November 13, 2009.

We ended up being oversold by *$2 billion*. The demand was for 100 million shares—our plan had been to sell *8* million. Some buyers wanted 100,000 shares, and we only could allot them 5,000–10,000 shares.

Our stock price was supposed to open at $15–$16. It came out at $19. A half hour after we were on the market, as we watched anxiously to see how investors would respond, the price jumped to $23.50.

It didn't stop there. Our third-quarter comp store sales increased nearly 14 percent—an almost ridiculous number, especially during a recession and retail downturn.

On Friday the thirteenth (of all dates) of November 2009, I stood with my team at the Nasdaq MarketSite in Times Square, the world-famous location of the New Year's Eve ball drop. Instead of ringing in a new year, we were there to ring the opening bell of that day's trading. Our Cinderella story was about to become complete.

In front of the Nasdaq MarketSite on November 13, 2009.

I can't adequately describe just how great a feeling it was to press that button and to achieve something very few people, if any, believed we could achieve.

Imagine seeing your name several stories high in the middle of New York's Times Square: "Nasdaq Welcomes Bob Fisch, chief executive officer, rue21." Right below that, it read, "Do You rue? I Do! Nasdaq."

Immediately following rue21's IPO victory celebration at Nasdaq, *John Megrue*, CEO of Apax Partners US—who later became cochair of *Bridgewater Associates*, the world's largest hedge fund—sent this handwritten note to me:

*Your leadership of rue exemplifies generosity, integrity, leadership, heart, soul and love … you attract amazing talent and set a tone of "we must win" "we will win" and "we will win together." You, and [your team], will tell future generations of this moment. You are an inspiration to everyone, including me.*

Less than two months after we hit the market, rue21's share price was $31, double the predicted opening price.

The *Vision* of a *New Retail Reality* that I had invested rue21's future in, with *Confidence*, culminated in twin peaks of validation: first, the 2009 IPO; second, the valuation of rue21 at $1.1 billion when it was sold, in 2013, to private equity firm Apax.

The *New Retail Reality* proved to be the powerful engine of unprecedented growth that, at its height, made rue21 a darling of Wall Street.

# CHAPTER TWELVE

# WHAT MOTIVATES YOU?

**I'm a big sports guy, and I am fascinated by streaks.** Maybe the mother of all streaks is *Cal Ripken's* mind-boggling record of playing in 2,632 consecutive games with the *Baltimore Orioles*. That means he did not miss a single game in seventeen years!

As for me, I didn't miss a day of work from 1978 to 2016. That's thirty-eight straight years. I made sure that I got sick only on weekends. If that sounds like a joke, it's not. The subconscious is very powerful. If you convince your body it needs to keep going, you'd be surprised how well it responds to the power of suggestion.

Like Cal Ripken, going to work made me feel better. Most people never got sick who worked for me, except for one senior management executive who broke down some Mondays and Fridays.

Another remarkable streak is *Joe DiMaggio*'s brilliant consistency hitting safely in fifty-six consecutive baseball games with the *New York Yankees*. If that doesn't sound like a big deal, consider that Joltin' Joe did that in 1941, and no player has matched his achievement in nearly eighty years.

At rue21, one of my proudest accomplishments—as it would be for any CEO—was the performance streak that we achieved: we never missed a profit and sales projection for eleven straight years—forty-five straight quarters.

## MOTIVATOR-IN-CHIEF

That's an extraordinary record in any category of retailing. Nobody realistically expects it to happen. During that decade-plus stretch, we were a high-growth company, which means our projections were aggressive. That made the achievement even more gratifying.

Each quarter that we met the guidance motivated me further to keep the streak going for the following quarter, and the quarter after that, and so on. Nobody had to push me. I was the one who pushed everybody to keep it going.

I enjoy being the motivator-in-chief because I know that's the way things get done, get done on time, and get done well.

Not everybody is a leader or needs to be. But successful leaders can't rely on someone else to motivate them. Neither can good followers. If you are not naturally a self-starter, it's okay if you need others at first to prod you. After a while, though, your initiative and ambition should take over, so that you push yourself to get things done, exceed expectations, and eventually can push others to fulfill their potential. *Mutual Mentoring* also works between peers, not just between generations.

Everything we do in life and in work begins and ends with the same word: *Motivation.* Without that, we wouldn't get anywhere, and we wouldn't care.

It's like there's a motor inside our brain that sends signals to our body, which then follows the "head" guy's orders like a good soldier.

We decide how fast the motor runs, where we want it to take us—and how far. For some people, the motor never stops running. Even when we're asleep, our subconscious motor is chugging away in overdrive. When it's time to wake up, we jump up, full of ideas and energy, ready to attack the day and make things happen. That describes me to a T. My philosophy always has been, "The sky is the limit. You can maneuver the universe."

Here's a short list of some things that motivate me:

- Knowing I can make a difference motivates me.

- Sharing my knowledge motivates me.

- Pushing people to succeed motivates me.

- Surrounding myself with smart, hardworking people motivates me.

- Defying the odds motivates me.

- Proving others wrong when they doubt me, or try to undermine or demean me, motivates me.

(What motivates *you*? I'd love to see your list.)

Let's look at that last one for a moment. When I was just learning the ropes of retailing at Abraham & Straus, one of my bosses told me, "I don't see you getting a merchant position in sportswear. I see you being only in boys' or in men's. You don't have a taste level for fashion."

He may as well have lit a fire under me, literally. That's the effect a comment like that has on me. It's a dare, a challenge, to prove the person wrong.

Not that he knew it at the time, but my A&S boss did me a favor with his insulting remark. He turned up the flame on that fire already burning inside me.

Almost twenty years later, I saw him at an Abraham & Straus reunion. He still was a store manager. I was president of Casual Corner, a major specialty sportswear chain. I guess I was more motivated to get ahead than he was.

I've met several people like that person, who thought they could push me around. I've never hesitated to shove them right back, twice as hard as they pushed me, to put them in their rightful place. I've never failed to take their remarks as fuel for my fire. I was totally motivated to make sure that, if anyone was going to get burned, it wasn't going to be me.

## THE CEO FROM CENTRAL CASTING

I learned my lessons the hard way. That's usually the best way, I've found, because you don't forget. They stick with you forever.

When I was a young merchandise manager at Jordan Marsh Miami, there was one time when I was being set up. I knew it. I could see it.

The person I reported to felt threatened by my aggressiveness. I was called into the office of chairman and CEO **Bill Rubin**. This man had the classic look of a chairman. In the apparel retail business, he was an icon who commanded respect throughout the industry.

In the room with him was Jordan Marsh president **Bruce Burnham**. They told me the dress category, to which I recently had

# DON'T DOUBT YOURSELF JUST BECAUSE OTHERS MIGHT

To help **Millennials** I'm mentoring become more motivated and productive, I share with them inspiring stories, especially of sports figures.

Take **Baker Mayfield**. He virtually willed himself to be a superstar athlete. As a football quarterback in high school, he wasn't recruited by big-name colleges. One reason was his height: six-foot-one isn't that big among today's towering quarterbacks. No problem, thought Mayfield.

Without being invited, the Texas native walked on the field to try out for Texas Tech. He not only made the squad; he became the first *freshman* to start a season-opening game for a major college football team.

After winning the coveted Heisman Trophy as the nation's top collegiate football player, he was the number-one overall pick in the 2018 NFL Draft, joining the Cleveland Browns, a team that had gone without a win the previous season.

What motivates Baker Mayfield? He says, "I hate losing more than I love winning." Mayfield's secret weapon is a fierce determination to prove himself.

If anyone has what it takes to lead the Browns back to respectability, it's Baker Mayfield. In his rookie season leading the team at quarterback, the formerly winless Browns gained instant credibility by winning almost half their games.

been assigned as merchandise manager, was underperforming. They questioned whether I was the right person to turn that business around.

I remember the sight of Bill Rubin pounding on his desk as he spoke. I also remember the desk. It was beautiful: a big oval piece of oak furniture that I couldn't take my eyes off. The whole scene was intimidating, like something out of a movie. This distinguished executive was sitting at his throne like he was master of the universe. I liked that. I wanted that.

At the same time, I stayed focused and on topic. I told them I had identified the central problem that had to be solved: our inventory was down 25 percent. They told me to come back when I had it figured out. I started crunching numbers.

Two weeks later, as they had instructed, I went back to show them my plan. I had charted the inventory levels, by store, that we needed for the next three months. It was my chance to prove I was the best person for the job, and they went with it.

I was fortunate to have Bruce as my mentor. He took me under his wing, and said he would look out for me, but only if I met our projections for both profit margin and total sales. I assured him I would.

Over the next two years, I did just that. My dress numbers in profit and sales were the strongest throughout not only Jordan Marsh, but also across all department store dress divisions of our parent company, Allied Stores. They had given me the inventory I wanted, and I gave them the sales and margin we needed.

After Bill Rubin left the company, I was promoted to general merchandise manager. Guess who ended up sitting at that big oval oak desk? That's right. At last, the desk I coveted was mine.

SCHOOL OF FISCH LESSON

## LEARN TO LIKE TOUGH LOVE

It's not unusual to feel intimidated by a mentor or boss who is confrontational. I get it. I've been there. Someone gets in your face and ratchets up the pressure. No matter what anybody says to you, don't stop busting your butt. Like me, you might find yourself climbing right over that person on your way up the ladder.

The more demanding a boss, the more motivated you'll be to prove you can take it to the next level. It's more likely to make *you* a strong leader than working for someone easy to please.

People and productivity thrive on creative tension. Friction fires up people, and fire is a source of energy.

Whether you're a **Millennial**, Gen Z, Gen X, or even **Baby Boomer**, it's healthy to welcome all kinds of feedback—sometimes it's encouraging other times it's a wake-up call to fix a problem. Savor the experience. Make it work for you, not against you.

*If you fight hard enough for what you want, and show you are right, you will get what you want.*

It's standard office politics. Either you get good at infighting or you end up as roadkill. I was very confident and charged ahead constantly, which didn't suit everybody's taste.

My controversial reputation motivated me. If being edgy and unorthodox helps a business succeed, I won't hesitate doing **Whatever It Takes**, and letting the chips fall where they may.

You have to show people what you can do and put your reputation on the line. Taking that risk to prove yourself is part of the motivation. Without risk, there's no reward.

Some people make the same mistakes every place they work instead of learning from them. I took what I learned at one job experience and carried it to the next experience. I studied the **Pieces of the Puzzle**. My victories at rue21 were in part the result of what I learned at Casual Corner. Everything is connected.

You have so many chances to do good things and to feel good about them. The key is not to let things happen to you, but to make them happen because of you. I believe almost everybody can do it if they put their minds to it. My focus is to keep others focused. That's my primary definition of leadership: knowing everybody's business to push them to the next level, so they don't get distracted.

If you let it distract you every time someone has a harsh criticism, you're depriving yourself of the opportunity to learn and to grow. Tough love makes you tougher, and that's a good thing. Don't take it personally. Confront your struggles now, and you'll thank yourself in the future. That is what should motivate you.

# CHAPTER THIRTEEN

# LISTENING

## How well do you *Listen* to other people?

Listening sounds like an easy thing to do. It isn't. People don't hear things well, or don't want to. You have to work to get better at it.

I owe the idea for this chapter to **Steve Richter**, a financial analyst I met at a Columbia University retail conference. Steve suggested that a chapter on **Listening** would be both pertinent and persuasive. He pointed out that, in our current noise-filled world, the ability to *Listen* has become broader and more complex.

Steve noted that the smartest people often don't speak a lot. They *Listen* to others speak. I thought about what he said. Ten months later, when I spoke to Steve, I told him the book would include a chapter on *Listening*, as he advised. He couldn't believe I remembered him telling me that.

*Listening* is essential to our growth as thinking, productive human beings. It also is complicated. It enables us to better understand each other and to better take in helpful information.

When done right, in a way that will help you succeed, *Listening* is active. It can make a powerful connection with people. You need to constantly stay alert. If you're a passive listener, you may hear what's being said, but that's not enough. We should *Listen* to what makes sense, while we dismiss what sounds inauthentic.

Questioning what you hear is part of *Listening*. So is challenging what you hear. *Listening* is learning. It's seeing things in a new light, through other people's eyes. Sometimes, it's the people who speak the least who know the most. They spend most of their time *Listening* and accumulating information.

I'm amazed when people don't take advantage of *Listening* to learn something.

The anecdotes throughout this book vary in time, place, and situation, but they all have something in common, something that helped me keep moving up the career ladder I designed for myself: I *Listened* very intently to what others said. The more you focus on it, the better you become at it.

I know for certain there were times when people I managed assumed that I wasn't *Listening* when they were talking to me. Many people will tell you I didn't *Listen*, but I really did! This whole book is about me *Listening*. I didn't always say, "I understand" or "I hear you." But, I always heard them, even if people didn't think I always was *Listening*. If I wasn't, I wouldn't have been able to accomplish what I did.

# LEARN To LISTEN CRITICALLY

By *Listening* analytically to what people said, I was able to make better decisions, because I took into account all points of view.

When I was at US Shoe Corp., running Casual Corner, I wanted to more aggressively increase our presence in outlet centers. But there was a difference of opinion in the ranks. The senior VP of real estate for US Shoe Corp. was convinced that outlets would begin to flatten out as a growth segment.

He was right. If we stuck with my original plan, it could have hurt the company's growth curve—and reflected poorly on me. Instead, we focused on our strip center and value mall locations. Making that pivot was a key piece of the puzzle that helped me build rue21.

It doesn't mean I always received sound advice. Being selective in how you *Listen*, and who you *Listen* to, is critical. Learn to filter out bad advice. *Listening* to the wrong advice or to misinformation can turn dangerous. It takes some practice to learn to detect that the people talking maybe don't know what they're talking about, or have a hidden agenda that is at cross purposes with your best interests.

## LEARN BY LISTENING

There always are opportunities for *Listening*, which takes different forms. It can be a casual conversation or an argument. *Listening* can be two way when others are involved, or it can be one way. Reading is a form of *Listening*. So is going to a seminar.

When I attended retailing or investment conferences, I made it a point to sit in on talks by other retailers. Why wouldn't I want to keep track of what they were doing and saying? I figured I might also pick up some ideas in the process. Maybe I would hear something that would help me better compete in the marketplace.

That all sounds logical, right? You would think other CEOs would do the same: keep close tabs on the pulse of the marketplace simply by sitting in a meeting room during a business session. But very few of them did what I did. I'm not sure why. Maybe they thought they knew it all, or that they knew enough to get by, or that they just didn't have the time to spare.

I think just the opposite. You need to make the time. You can never know enough, let alone know too much. The more you know, the better you'll perform and the more successful you'll be.

When kicking around ideas, even casually, you definitely should keep a record of what was said. It's also smart and helpful to record and retain someone's personal interests, likes, and dislikes. You never know when that intimate information can come in handy to help you form a bond that benefits your business interests.

It's not always about getting ahead. It may not be an action point that you hear. It can be more abstract, such as background information. How to file it away quickly? It's easy enough to make a voice note on your phone or type in a few words immediately after hearing something. If you have paper and pen nearby, use that. You don't need to write a lot, just two to three items or ideas to jog your memory.

# HOW TO WEAPONIZE LISTENING

You can weaponize **Listening**. Let's say you are dealing with people inside your own company—a boss, for example, or, in my case, a board of directors. Whomever I was dealing with, I made a point of using my **Listening** powers to move the company ahead.

I remember the time the CEO of US Shoe Corp., **Phil Barach**, stunned one of my senior executives, Perry Bugnar. He simply asked Perry about his wife and kids—by name. Perry couldn't believe the big boss would remember the names of one person's family members in a company of thousands.

Phil's "secret" was that he always would write down such details after first meeting someone. That concern for each individual creates a powerful personal connection that leaves a big impression. He was being an empathetic **Listener**. Being a good leader is more than crunching numbers. It's important to get inside people's heads to understand and fulfill their needs.

If you don't already do it, get in the habit of writing down notes right after a conversation. I picked up that habit from Phil, and it's worked out very well all these years in helping me bond with people.

## NO BACK-SEAT LISTENERS

The personal touch reaches beyond business too. Part of the legacy of *Senator John McCain* is his insistence on treating everybody with equal respect and dignity, no matter their station in life. Being curious and interested in others leads to asking questions and to *Listening* more closely.

McCain made it a habit of sitting in the front passenger seat when he hired professional drivers. I like to send birthday greetings to the drivers. I invited one of the regular drivers to rue21's IPO.

I found that was a consistently effective way to work with people. *Listening* helped me plan a meeting of rue21's board of directors. I started visualizing how the meeting would go, based on the points of discussion on the agenda.

In my mind, for a board meeting to be considered productive and successful, I needed to understand what all board members were thinking. I would play out in my mind how I wanted the meeting to go. That careful preparation, however, did not start a week before the meeting. It sometimes started three to six months earlier.

Here is where both your memory and your note-taking discipline come into play. At a board meeting, I would bring up initiatives from the prior board meeting—ones I knew board members might have favored.

People tend to not remember things they told you six months ago. My reliance on that quirk of human behavior always helped me get ahead.

When you need the approval of others on an ambitious plan that you are eager to execute, don't say to the other stakeholders, "Here is what I'm going to do," and then act as if they only need to rubber-stamp your plan of action. That comes across as too cocky. It only makes decision makers nervous. Do not go to a meeting thinking that you already have permission to do whatever you want.

I always want to know what others are thinking. Sometimes you pick that up not in the words they say, but in what I think of as *silent vibrations*. You need to strike a careful balance between **Listening** and pushing your agenda. Have you ever attempted this approach? If not, try it!

Business isn't the only place where **Listening** can give you what you want. The same approach works in personal situations. Take social media. You may not think of Instagram or other platforms as places where you **Listen** to others, but you can pick up details there about someone's personal interests and experiences that can be used to develop a more empathetic relationship with them, whether it's platonic or even romantic.

## OTHER PEOPLE'S LIVES

We communicate with each other through social media, and subconsciously reveal ourselves, in many ways, through the images and comments we share. If we **Listen** carefully to what our connections post, we might be able to learn as much about them as if we were having an intimate conversation.

It's common courtesy to pay attention to what people tell you about their lives, whether it's verbally or through images and text. Anyone who is active on social media is there because they want the attention and engagement of others, just as if they were speaking to you in person.

They might be speaking or posting about their children, their favorite vacation spot, or which sports team they root for. Tidbits of information like that come in handy when you're trying to ingratiate yourself with someone for business, personal, or other reasons.

To become a world-class **Listener**, you need to be a student of human nature. At the same time that I *Listen* to other people, I also pay attention to how they act. You can't be naïve about it.

When I first arrived at rue21, one senior director complained to me about someone who reported to her. I was told that the person in question was inconsistent in showing up to work on time.

I *Listened* to the senior director, who I could tell was in over her head and was shifting blame to this other person. When I spoke to her assistant, I heard a different story altogether. As I *Listened* to her version of events, I could tell she was a *Genuine* person who really cared about the success of rue21. The outcome is that she went on to a long and successful career at the company, while her boss was gone within a few weeks.

If two people give you two contradictory points of view about the same situation, who do you *Listen* to? That's what separates *Listening* from hearing. With *Listening*, there is context to consider. You know by people's previous actions how they operate.

Your gut instinct should tell you something as well. It's as if you need to hone your instincts into a lie detector that can distinguish between someone telling the truth and bending, if not ignoring, the truth.

The central purpose and benefit of careful *Listening* is to see things from other people's perspectives and not just your own. If you only *Listen* to yourself all the time, it creates an "echo chamber," and that's not healthy.

There were times when I saw that people made a concerted effort not to *Listen*. The reason was obvious: they didn't like what they were hearing, so they shut out the unwelcome news. When some associates at Casual Corner wanted to know where their profit-sharing checks were, I told them we did not achieve a profit last year.

Their reaction was, "We always get them at the end of the year." You can talk to someone until you're out of breath, but you can't make them *Listen* if they put up a mental block.

## ARE YOU LISTENABLE?

The converse of being a good *Listener* is being good at *getting people to Listen to you.*

When I took over at rue21, which was in a turnaround situation, I was determined to have our company taken seriously by manufacturers. We needed their respect and full attention to become as successful as I knew we could be. You have to fight for what you want. You cannot be shy about it, and, fortunately, it's not my nature to be timid. I am very up-front about what I want and what I expect of others.

When I arrived at rue21, it was immediately obvious to me that it didn't have the respect it deserved. I was determined to change that, and the rest of the team I was building followed my lead going forward. When you believe in yourself and your business, and focus on fulfilling your potential, you are on the way to becoming the best you can be. rue21 was on the way to becoming the best in class.

If I heard that my merchants were kept waiting at a manufacturer's showroom, that was my cue to go right to the top. I didn't need an appointment. I did need to stand up for my merchant team. I went right into the company owner's office. I simply reminded the owner that we were buying millions of dollars of goods. Then, after making my point, what I did *not* do is give the owner an ultimatum. That's the wrong approach.

To get the owner to *Listen*, I stated a fact: I reminded him or her how much money rue21 spent with the company.

What I didn't have to spell out was that if we pulled our business, the manufacturer's business would suffer seriously. I didn't say that, but I made sure that the message was heard—loud and clear.

I then would ask: "Can my people walk in here any time and be seen immediately?" The answer invariably was, "Absolutely. We will treat you as our most important customer."

After that, we never had a problem receiving excellent service when we visited a showroom. It was important for the industry to respect all facets of our business—finance, store operations, marketing, and every other area. I had to take control to shape that perception, so the people we dealt with in the industry would respect our company and our team.

In the same sense, I also wanted to get the attention of FedEx, the shipping company rue21 used. I did the logical thing: I contacted the CEO directly. He came to my office to assure me the company valued our business and would provide us top-quality service. At that early point in my tenure, rue21 was not yet a force in the marketplace.

Acting like you *are* big is how you *get* big! After that meeting with the CEO, we enjoyed great service from FedEx. I found a way that he would *Listen* to what I had to

## Acting like you are big is how you get big!

say. He *Listened* and acted on it.

Even though FedEx Ground was a $15 billion company, and we were a $100 million company, I had no hesitation reaching out to its CEO. Always ensure you go to the people at the top who are the decision makers. Don't settle for anything less, no matter what position you hold.

That's the attitude I used to build this business. We weren't afraid to stand up and go directly to decision makers. That's a key *Piece of the Puzzle*. When the people you deal with on a daily basis are fully aware you've spoken to the top person, it totally changes their view of who you are and the level of customer service you receive. You are guaranteed to get VIP treatment.

For business and personal travel, I am a frequent flier on a private airline service called *JetSmarter*. There were certain customer service issues that I wanted to bring to the attention of the CEO and founder, **Sergey Petrossov**. At the same time, I had recommendations for improvements, based on my decades of experience both in business and as a customer of the company.

After reading a piece he wrote in the JetSmarter newsletter, I could see Sergey was a **Millennial** with great **Vision** who is determined to build a unique business model in the airline industry. I wanted to meet him. I emailed him my thoughts, which echoed some of his own observations in the article he had written. The upshot was that Sergey invited me to his office to talk further about how to improve JetSmarter's service and business.

Sergey was bright and compassionate. We discussed how to build trust and improve communications. I was able to bring to bear my skills to offer him the perspective of a customer with deep management expertise. I wanted to see him succeed.

The best *Listening* situations occur when there is mutual respect between two people. That was the case with **Tom Unrine**, executive vice president of US Shoe Corp. when I worked there. Prior to that, Tom was head merchant at Jordan Marsh, when I worked for its parent company, Federated Department Stores. Tom was instrumental in helping me relate better to people from different backgrounds than mine. His criticism that I could come across to some people as arrogant was constructive and well intended. I *Listened* to him and adjusted my approach, as he suggested. It worked. People responded to me more positively because I had *Listened* to Tom's advice.

What Tom taught me about properly dealing with people and staying calm even in stressful situations helped me a great deal at the time, and for the rest of my life. It wasn't hard for someone to read my opinion of them through my facial expressions—whether good, bad, or indifferent. In sharp contrast to me, Tom always kept a poker face. You wouldn't know for sure if he loved you or hated you. He taught me to make people feel important, which helped me hone my *Listening* skills.

Tom is one of the **Mentors** I respect now more than ever. Each type has its own set of *Listening* dynamics.

## HOW WE LISTEN DIFFERS BY SPEAKER

With parents or other relatives, the arc of how you *Listen* changes from childhood to adulthood. When young, even if you don't like what you hear, and even though you may groan about it, you generally do what you're told. (The same can be said about *Listening* to teachers.) When you grow into an adult, you decide independently of your parents whether what you hear is agreeable and whether you will act on it or reject it.

Equally important is how to make sure your supervisors *Listen* to your ideas, your updates, or anything else you are talking about in their presence. If you notice the telltale signs of someone not *Listening* to you—minimal to no eye contact, frequent interruptions before you're finished, impatient body language, asking the same question more than once because they didn't *Listen* to your first answer—you've got work to do, my friend, especially if that someone is your boss.

The less a boss *Listens*, the more important it is that you find out why that's happening. The more bosses like what they hear, the more they will let you do what you want, and the more opportunity for advancement.

I base my decision to take action or not to take action on two primary factors: the strength of the information I hear and the strength of the speaker delivering it. The more experience and success that people have in a particular area, the more closely and curiously I will *Listen* to what they have to say because they are proven thought leaders in that area. At the same time, don't be fooled by surface charisma. Someone can sound impressive, but personal magnetism doesn't mean mastery of a subject.

Throughout I have mentioned my number-one rule of retailing: *Listen* to the customer! Had I not done that, there would be no rue21 success story to tell. It's not unique to rue21, nor to retailing. It's true for any business. There's a good reason the old expression, "The customer is always right," has endured through the years. Not *Listening* to the customer is not wanting to succeed. Anybody who worked for me who didn't understand that, or didn't live by it, didn't end up working for rue long.

In today's technology-obsessed culture, we *Listen* to all sorts of things, but not necessarily to each other. *Millennials* are big fans of podcasts, as are people of all ages. Like music, podcasts can go anywhere with us. We can enjoy a novel, become more informed from news analysis, or learn from business advice—all while driving, walking, eating, or working. That's convenient, but it also can be distracting. Does it encourage constructive thinking, or does it get in the way of freeing your mind to create new ideas and goals?

I see a connection between the common behavior of staying plugged in all the time and the difficulty some *Millennials* have holding a lengthy conversation without being easily distracted or inattentive.

## FOCUS ON NOT BEING DISTRACTED

I'd like to see *Millennials* become better *Listeners*. Not to generalize unfairly, but in my experience over the years, I've seen some *Millennials* become too easily distracted, whether it's a phone or other shiny object capturing their attention. They are texting while someone is leading a meeting, or they are talking and texting during meals. You know the drill.

*Millennials* also could be more receptive to constructive criticism. Being critical is not a negative. To me, it means the person criticizing really cares about wanting to make somebody better. A good leader does not say, "Hey, you're doing really well," then walk away and not monitor ongoing performance. It's just as unacceptable to be negatively critical without productively mentoring and nurturing the person.

## Being critical is not a negative.

I went to our *Millennial Advisory Board (MAB)* to listen to members' thoughts on the importance of *Listening*. *Nicole Campbell* and *Desiree "Dezz" Nunes* weighed in.

"*Listening* is a big topic," Dezz said. "In the workforce, where I always try to learn new skill sets, *Listening* is one of the hardest. You're often thinking about what to say next before the other person finishes speaking.

"I like to *Listen* to people and learn about them," she added. "When talking with friends, for instance, I'll want to interject right away, but I try to be conscious of it and save my thoughts until they are finished. The problem is that if you wait to respond, you might forget, but I try hard to let people talk. They like to tell stories, so I do my best to *Listen* and respond. Some people have to put a lot of effort into *Listening* and paying attention and hearing. I'm naturally very curious, so it comes easier to me."

Dezz said she sees how well someone is *Listening* from the other person's eye contact, body language, and reaction. "There are signs of engagement I do look for, like if they are nodding in agreement."

Nicole tells of an unnerving experience she had at a business social event while talking to a woman who clearly was not *Listening* to anything she was saying. "She was so distracted, she must have asked me, 'How are you?' five times within a few minutes. I see that more and more in the workplace."

On a separate occasion, Nicole was having a bite to eat with someone who was on her phone the entire time they were together at the table. "People are so self-centered," Nicole observed. She said that when people do squeeze bits of conversation in between getting their digital fix, there's no time to reflect on what was said because "it's back to the phone right away. It's really a disease today."

Nicole doesn't consider what she calls the "epidemic of social isolation and distraction" to be "a *Millennial* thing." She sees it in *Boomers* and in people of all ages. "We have a crisis of information overload," she observed. "We're so incredibly distracted because we get information thrown at us. There's a lot of consuming of content, but really not a lot of *Listening*. It's everyone, not just *Millennials*. *Listening* no longer is a must-have, but a nice-to-have. When people do *Listen*, that's the superpower." To succeed, you absolutely need it.

How does Dezz strive to make sure she is heard in her workplace? "When I'm communicating to clients, I try to do a better job of communicating in a clear and concise way," she said. "Sometimes, people go off on a tangent and give out too much information that's not relevant. I've found it's better to shorten what you say; make it concise and captivating. Sometimes, less is more. You engage people more when you say a little less. You try to get them to participate in the conversation."

## LISTEN BETWEEN THE LINES

Nicole's approach to engaging *Listeners* is to "understand what their goals and problems are. It's first knowing what they want." She acknowledged it's not always so easy to get that information. "People are so busy and distracted, it's hard to get them to sit down and have a conversation so you can get to that deep understanding."

One way that Nicole works around that challenge is to "listen between the lines." She explained that she tries to "understand what's not being said and what is motivating that person. You apply that empathy and put yourself in their shoes. It lets you connect the dots and be more powerful in your findings by *Listening.*"

Dezz had an interesting—and, I think, a very valid—perspective on my comment about *Millennials* not seeming to accept criticism willingly and not paying undivided attention when engaged in conversation, whether it's business or personal.

She attributes that to her generation being more confrontational as a whole than *Baby Boomers* or *Generation X*. I agree that *Millennials* have, as she put it, "shaken things up from how things used to work and how the world traditionally has been."

Dezz added, "My parents or their parents maybe were taught to be nonconfrontational and wanted to make things work and keep things going forward. I don't feel opinions were as openly discussed as they are now. *Millennials* are *Disruptors*. We're not afraid to express ourselves. As a result of that mentality, maybe we're not always the best *Listeners*. We're anxious to get our thoughts out."

Nicole and Dezz are especially vibrant members of the *Millennial* generation, and of our own *Millennial Advisory Board*. They give me hope that there's a lot of room to meet in the middle between the generations, as long as we constantly are striving to *Listen* to each other respectfully, closely, and curiously.

# CHAPTER FOURTEEN

# THE BEST IS YET TO COME

## "Retirement" is a word you'll never hear me use, at least not in reference to myself.

It wasn't always like that, though. I had my own great awakening that, in a sense, both saved my career and catapulted it to a level I never dared imagine possible.

In my late forties, I was at US Shoe, running Casual Corner & Co., when the new owner, Claudio Del Vecchio, asked me one day about my goals for the future. It's a fair question, the type you might get asked in a job interview.

When I told Claudio that I was thinking of retiring in my early fifties, he looked at me as if to say, "Why do I want this guy to work for me if he has no ambition?" It was true that I had grown complacent, and it didn't escape his attention. At one point, he even poked a little fun at my having put on a few pounds, but he was making a point. And he wasn't wrong.

I wasn't happy, mostly because it was hard for me to get excited about what the new owners wanted me to do. I thought it was the wrong strategy. I had what I believed were bigger and better plans, but Claudio and his father, Leonardo, were the owners, so it was their way or the highway.

Looking back, I was foolish to tell him I wanted to retire at fifty-two. I'm not sure what I was thinking. The wrong words just fell out of my mouth, at the wrong time.

In my final days at US Shoe, Claudio wished me well, expressing confidence that I would have a strong career ahead. That was kind of him to say. Over the next year of job hunting, though, there were moments when I found that prediction hard to believe. I wondered and worried about the kind of future I would have.

For the first time in my working life, I wasn't working. If this is what retirement's like, I said to myself, no, thank you! It was no fun at all. It wasn't relaxing in the least.

I constantly was looking, interviewing, talking to headhunters, and soul searching. It was a blessing in that it made me realize I never wanted to be in that position again, retirement or otherwise. Some of the encounters with headhunters were humiliating.

When you're in a job, they treat you like gold. When you're in between jobs, they treat you like garbage. It's like being swept into the corner when the housekeeper comes, and you don't know where to go. You find yourself hanging out somewhere for a couple of hours in between appointments with nothing to do. It's a cold, empty, scary feeling.

## JUST GETTING STARTED

I had earned my first CEO position at thirty-seven, running TH Mandy for US Shoe Corp. By most measures, reaching the C-suite is the peak of a career in business. I didn't see it that way, though. I didn't say to myself, "I've made it!" No way. I still had a lot to learn to continue putting together the *Pieces of My Puzzle.*

As fulfilling as it was to take Casual Corner & Co. to approximately 300 stores, from three, I never considered that the culmination of my retail career. I was just getting started. There was much more I wanted and needed to do to fulfill my *Vision* and my ambitions. I knew full well I had a long way still to go.

I had met with nearly twenty prospective employers after leaving US Shoe. I did get offers, but not anything that appealed to me. Even though it was tough to be on the sidelines, I also was not going to settle and take just anything that came along. I was following my own rule about taking a stand, waiting for the ideal opportunity.

Going through that uncomfortable period helped change my perspective on retirement. It clarified for me what kind of position I wanted to fill next. Yes, it humbled me, but it also made me determined to stick it out.

Then something clicked. An executive I knew at *Charlotte Russe, Bernie Zeichner,* suggested that I speak with the equity firm that controlled rue21.

The retail chain had all kinds of challenges, and it would be an uphill battle. Other than the confidence I had in my own abilities, there were no guarantees it would work. Despite the odds facing me, I was eager and excited to begin again.

Why would I want a formidable challenge like that at fifty-one years old, after almost thirty years of working?

*Bob Grayson* is a big part of the answer. He was a major influence on my decision to go for it. Bob was a consultant to rue21 who previously had been president of *Lerner Shops* and *The Limited*, where he worked for legendary merchant *Leslie Wexner*.

"Do you really want this job?" Bob asked me. "You're in your fifties ... you've been extremely successful. To do this, you can't fly fifty thousand feet in the air and go on autopilot. To do this job right, you have to be in the bushes to succeed."

His blunt talk switched on a light in my head. The bushes! That's where I wanted to be!

It all crystallized for me at that moment. I was coming off a year of roaming in the wilderness. That experience gave me a heightened appreciation for the rare opportunity I was being handed: to build a business almost from scratch.

I'm not the type who likes to float above it all, taking it easy just because I already had a long career. I want to be in the thick of it. I'm much more comfortable leaning forward than I am leaning back.

At US Shoe, I wasn't finding the right *Pieces of the Puzzle* to fit in the next chapter of my career. So, a year after leaving US Shoe, at the ripe young age of fifty-one, I became CEO of rue21. I had finally found the next piece.

By time I went to work for rue21, I was obsessed and hungry to be alive and working. I had lost a lot of weight. It changed me. From that point on, for the next fifteen years, I saw rue21 through its explosive period of growth.

## AN ADVENTURE, NOT A JOURNEY

Regardless of my age, my mindset hasn't changed. I want to keep going … and going … and going. Why stop? For me, life isn't merely a journey. That sounds too passive to me. Life is meant to be an adventure, full of surprises and personal fulfillment. I still haven't stopped learning. In fact, the best years for me have been my fifties and sixties.

When I want to sit and watch as a spectator, I'll go to a Yankees game or a Broadway show. Otherwise, I want to be like that player on the field, or the performer on the stage, making things happen, stimulating people, getting them excited about their own adventure.

How about you?

If you're not prepared to enthusiastically answer that question affirmatively, my goal is to move you closer to that answer by the time you finish reading this book.

In my years of working with *Millennials*, I've become concerned about what I see. Many *Millennials* seem to think they're peaking in their thirties. It's all too tempting today to look outward at the world, and give in to external forces, letting them control our state of mind and our actions.

As I said in chapter 13, with relentless and pervasive media distractions fighting for our attention, we have to work harder to stay within ourselves and true to our values.

It's not an easy thing to do. It takes a lot of willpower and focus to look inward, to decide for ourselves the best way to spend our time, and whom to spend it with.

## YOU HAVE TO SEE IT TO ACHIEVE IT

As you grow older (and hopefully wiser), you gain more clarity about what you want to do, and whom you *don't* want to spend your time with. You should always be assessing the value of your experiences and your relationships.

How do they all fit into your career arc? Everyone should want to climb the ladder to success and achieve the goals they set for themselves. Without goals, achievement is elusive. If you can't define what you want, you don't know what it looks like. If you can't see it, you can't achieve it.

Ever since that first day at A&S, I've had a burning desire to meet my goals. I still have that desire. One of the ways I keep focused is by learning to be more selfish with my time. Time is the most precious, and scarce, resource we have. Once it's gone, you won't get it back.

We always need to be asking ourselves the question, "What is in my best interests?" If that sounds self-centered, it needs to be, in this respect: you can't help, or relate positively to, other people unless you first have your own act together.

The fact you're reading this book is proof positive that you are ambitious and curious about how to improve your position in life as a professional and as a private individual.

What you do today with your time and the choices you make will determine how tomorrow treats you. Because I have experienced it myself, I strongly believe in the philosophy that *The Best Is Yet to Come*, but that happens only if you invest your *best* efforts in what you do here and now. That was my mindset at thirty-seven, and that is my mindset today. At forty years old, I felt *Fearless*, and I was confident that the best moments of my life lay ahead, well into the future.

# ATTACK LIFE AS AN ADVENTURE, NOT AN ANXIETY ATTACK

It's easy to get down on yourself. We all do it. Just don't beat yourself up about it. There's a difference between getting down on yourself, due to disappointment, and getting in your own way.

Anxiety is caused by two interrelated states of mind: high hopes and fear of failure. A popular **Millennial** theory about how to rid yourself of negative thoughts is Mel Robbins's 5-Second Rule. It states that you should act on a positive impulse immediately, within five seconds of thinking it, before you procrastinate or talk yourself out of doing it. If there is the slightest hesitation, count down from five to one and then spring into action!

Don't think about it. Like Nike says, just do it!

Where do you want to go?

2    Mel Robbins, "The Five Elements of the 5 Second Rule," Mel Robbins, April 25, 2018, https://melrobbins.com/blog/five-elements-5-second-rule.

No matter what challenges I faced in my professional life or personal life, I made it my business to always see the glass as half full. Optimism is a form of adrenaline or dopamine: it fills you up with self-generated energy that works like perpetual motion; it keeps pushing you ahead.

*The Best Is Yet to Come* does not refer strictly to monetary gain. It's tackling and completing what you enjoy. It's figuring out what fulfills you. It's creating a plan to pursue those pleasures, to fully enjoy the fruits of your labor.

Growth spurts can happen in your working life and your personal life at almost any time if conditions are right. You can continue to grow as long as you put your mind to it. That goes not just for *Millennials*.

When a *Gen Xer* I know turned fifty-one, he said to me, "If you had your best years after fifty, I guess I should start thinking like that too." In that instant, it was as if he began thinking of himself as a younger person, with new possibilities ahead. "I should start doing things!" he exclaimed.

## READY TO REVIVE, REINVENT, REBRAND

Decades ago, when *Baby Boomers* were in their *Millennial* phase as young adults, sixty-five was the standard retirement age. By that point, the average worker had been "on the job" for forty-plus years, and average life expectancy was considerably shorter than it is today.

After rue21, I was ready to revive, reinvent, rebrand, and write. I wasn't interested in resting on my laurels. It doesn't matter whether I'm working within a traditional corporate structure or creating my own structure, my attitude always is the same: *the work is never done.*

Once you lower your sights, you also lower your personal productivity, and you start to stagnate, feeling less fulfilled. I'm always thinking about what I can wrap my mind and my arms around next. In addition to advising CEOs and sitting on corporate boards, I'm reviewing a variety of projects related to this book—from seminars to podcasts to a *Fisch Tales* mentoring franchise. The busier, the better!

In my sixties, I was a mentor and speaker on career goals and leadership for three hundred members of the senior class at the *Fashion Institute of Technology* in New York City. The class had selected rue21 to study for its capstone retail project.

Famous fashion designer Tommy Hilfiger is another example of someone who experienced *The Best Is Yet to Come*. After some midcareer missteps lost him valuable market share, Tommy listened to smart advice from a *Mentor* and his business rebounded, better than ever.

After I turned fifty, I enjoyed by far my biggest success in life and business. Was I fortunate? No! I created my own good fortune. You can do that too.

So-called luck is the result of hard work and opportunity coming together in a perfect marriage. You make luck happen!

Let's take a look at some of the steps you can take to ensure for yourself that *The Best Is Yet to Come.*

If you don't already have a *Vision* of who you want to be, and what you want to do, try the alter ego exercise that's mentioned in chapter 11. We had an alter ego party, but you can simulate the same purpose of the party in private.

We all live in the moment, staying within our comfort zone. Imagining an ideal world—where you can be anybody you want and do whatever you want—requires stepping outside your comfort zone and assuming the alter ego of your idealized self. That's living outside the moment. It's living in the future. Stringing together those inside and out-of-body moments gives you *Momentum.*

Consider this example: the actor friend I mentioned in chapter 1 first was on stage in high school plays. He enjoyed it so much, he thought about pursuing the craft in college. He decided against it, though, and instead majored in journalism. After a long career in publishing, he started acting again, in local theater, as well as independent movies and commercials. He had resolved later in life to step out of his comfort zone as a writer and revisit his earlier aspirations, and he made it happen. In his mind, when it came to his acting ambitions late in life, he decided, "Who says the best isn't yet to come?"

Hiring managers sometimes ask job applicants, "Where do you want to be in five years?" The response they are looking for has less to do with the specific answer than with whether the candidate has thought that far ahead at all.

The importance of projecting what you want your future to look like cannot be overstated. What do you want to do with your life? Where do you want to go?

Many *Millennials* are more attuned to the present than to their future. Their short-term goal is to "make it" by, say, the age of thirty-five. What does "make it" mean, though? If it's just about money, that's already the wrong track to be on.

If "making it" means fulfilling your ambitions, following through on your passions, knowing your purpose, and wanting to give back through mentoring and volunteer work, I applaud your attitude, because you have the right one.

# HOW TO MAKE SURE THE BEST IS YET TO COME

Here is a sampling of the qualities and skills that will increase your odds that **The Best Is Yet to Come**.

**Instant Gratification.** It's an illusion. There are no shortcuts. If you sweat over your business plan, and surround yourself with the right people, your patience will be rewarded.

**Comfort Zone.** It's not your friend. Don't run from risks. Run toward them. Go on the offensive. Be ready to defend your position.

**Logic.** Don't overthink or trash a plan that sounds less than logical. Life isn't that predictable, and neither is business. Trust your gut.

**Tribal Knowledge**. The pedigree of a big-name company or college is nice, but give me anybody with street smarts, passion, and practical experience who works hard, and I'll give you growth and profits.

**Pieces of the Puzzle**. Know when it's time to move to the next rung on your career ladder. Don't keep a job past its useful life to you. Don't take a job that doesn't advance your career goals.

**Generation Generalizations**. Judge others (and yourself) on qualities such as **Vision**, ambition, and accomplishments, not as a cliché based on age.

**Stress**. It's not all bad. It stirs the blood. It means you care. It you don't like it, cure bad habits like procrastination.

**Purpose.** Pay it forward. Create a balance that ensures a healthy, happy life for yourself and your family, while it also contributes to the growth and happiness of others.

One of the strengths of the *Millennial* generation is the entrepreneurial streak that runs through its members. As with any generation, to a certain extent, *Millennials* are a product of their times.

Thanks to the democratization of digital technology, it's easier than ever to start your own business without incurring huge overhead or having to hire a large workforce. A lot of the infrastructure to conduct commerce today is readily accessible online.

If you have a good idea and the right business plan, you can leverage the virtual workplace to build a market for your product or service. That's another way to look at *The Best Is Yet to Come*. It refers also to the opportunities ahead as technology becomes more sophisticated, accessible, and cost efficient.

# CHAPTER FIFTEEN

# DO YOU rue?
# I (STILL) DO!

**By now, you know that this book, while it uses anecdotes and lessons from my career, is not meant to be a memoir.** It's meant to serve as a motivational tool, helping people navigate their own career ladder more purposefully, with fewer stumbles, by gleaning insights from my experiences.

Like *Mutual Mentoring*, the motivation runs both ways. It's not just from me to you. The more I can give back to *Millennials* and others as a result of my experiences, the more I get back in gratification, which spurs me on to new ideas and contributions.

During the course of writing *Fisch Tales*, when people asked me what the book is about, I would explain that my *mission* is to help *Baby Boomers* and *Millennials* better communicate and understand each other. This book is a written expression of that mission.

As anyone who's worked for me, or with me, will tell you, I'm on a mission every day of my life. Whatever task I take on—from planning a company awards dinner to running back and forth across the country to pitch an IPO—I dig into the details. I demand that every effort is made to meet and preferably to exceed expectations.

I'm not trying to make anyone's life difficult. Just the opposite. If people are pushed to do their best, their lives will be *less* difficult and more satisfying. Besides, I just couldn't live with myself if I didn't go all out with everything I do. I'm one of those people who won't ask a person to do something I won't do, or haven't previously done, myself.

That's a key point, because if someone says your expectations are unrealistic or unreasonable, your own direct experience is evidence that not only can it be done, but it *has* been done—by you!

To demand excellence in others is to care about their happiness and personal development. "Tough" can be a deceptive word, I find. It doesn't shock me that people think of me as tough. But you can be tough and tender at the same time. Toughness comes from passion, and passion comes from caring about how others perform and how they feel about their performance.

When everyone performs at a high level, then everyone benefits from a unified, consistent effort. It's not enough to excel in sporadic spurts. The ability to sustain consistently optimal effort is the difference between mediocre results and record-setting results.

## BEYOND THE NUMBERS

That is what enabled rue21 to become the largest specialty apparel retailer in store count in America. The sense of fulfillment that comes from a milestone of that scale is hard to describe adequately. Even so, store count, no matter how impressive, is a number, a statistic. It's data. And, if you've already read all the previous chapters of this book, you know by now how I feel about putting data on too tall a pedestal.

All the granular data in the world never will replace *Gut Instincts*, *Industry Knowledge*, *Experience*, and *Motivational Skills*, all of which prop up people to perform at their best.

I am not skeptical about the amazing new technology that will change the world, mostly for the better. Futuristic miracles like artificial intelligence need to happen. They're not substitutes, however, for the kind of tried-and-true data science I'm talking about.

If you want to talk data, I've been a data scientist in merchandise and marketing for more than forty years.

My job is to find the right product, put it in stores at the right time for the target audience, and make sure the stores know how to sell it. Whether you call it data science or *Tribal Knowledge*, the goal is to make an impact to exploit the business. You have to know how to merchandise, market, plan, and allocate.

One thing I know is how to build categories of business. Look at what we built with the accessories division etc!, which helped elevate rue21 to a public company.

I was successful because I was hands-on. I didn't have to be a great "picker" of styles. I knew that was not my primary strength. I made sure to develop and to hire retailers who built a proven track record of buying skills.

I became good at knowing how to exploit the categories for merchandising impact in our stores.

I paid close attention and then acted on what I saw. Going after new categories—whether it's reinventing yourself by adding lines of beauty, fragrance, or sandals—was *Putting It on the Line* to exploit

# DATA'S NOT A PANACEA

The kind of individual critical thinking that used to be standard operating procedure in fashion retailing is being replaced by number-crunching machines.

There's a shrinking pool of merchants who can crunch numbers in their head. It's become easier to rely on dry data that's automatically generated. The problem is that data alone can't teach someone to be a savvy merchant with **Tribal Knowledge** that is based on experience and intuition. There is no substitute for the human element.

Data understands patterns of behavior, which isn't really the same as understanding how people think. It isn't the same as understanding trends in taste. Analytics should be used to guide a merchant, not to take the place of product selection—unless you're selling to robots.

Analytics are not the whole answer. The answer is leveraging data-driven knowledge with well-trained merchants whose **Tribal Knowledge** turns data into dollars.

That's why I'm not big on "big data." I'm not advocating that you ignore it or minimize it. Just don't mistake it as a substitute for forming people into a tight-knit, championship-caliber team.

and build the business.

Like other **Baby Boomers**, I've had my share of achievements and, yes, some disappointments. On balance, the many adventures that formed my career have served me very well. Each **Piece of the Puzzle** in itself may not have met my high expectations, but once all the pieces started to fit together, at rue21 and afterwards, I could begin to appreciate that it was well worth the blood, sweat, and tears that I invested—and that others invested in me. That's a very big deal that cannot be overstated.

## IN PRAISE OF LOYAL PEOPLE ... LIKE STEPHANIE

Just as you need to place your **Trust** in those around you to achieve your goals, they have to **Trust** that you know what you're doing. And you must believe in your **Vision**.

I was fortunate to have loyal people close to me—my wife, Stephanie, not least among them—who made all the difference, particularly at those moments when I may have had doubts about what I was doing. Being around big-hearted, sincere people to boost you when you need it is more important than insincere people slapping you on the back when things are going great.

It's having not only the best and brightest people around you that matters to your success. It's having the most authentic (as in sincere) and passionate people, whose **Tribal Knowledge** matches your mission and your business plan.

Legacies are about what you leave behind and how it is perceived. It now is approaching two decades since I arrived at rue21. The legacy that makes me most proud, and, at the same time, most humble, is the family feeling that we built at rue21. Members of that family to this day are in contact, celebrating their own families' milestones with each other, comforting each other over their losses.

The culture of closeness and compassion that we created is rare. It is not something you find everywhere you work, so I don't take it for granted. I feel confident saying neither do other rue21 alumni.

The family bond that forms in a workplace cannot happen unless the leaders create a compatible environment for the interdependence to flourish. *That is what I am most proud of accomplishing at rue21.*

The links of a business fall apart when you don't care about people. Keep data in its bucket, and use it when you need to, but don't mistake it for the people factor that gives a company its character and personality. An overreliance on numbers can be numbing. There is no such thing as an overreliance on people.

At rue21, it was no secret how I felt about our associates. I never was too busy to spend quality time with anyone who needed an ear to bend or a shoulder to lean on. That's certainly an attitude that is not typical of most CEOs. The loyalty and dedication our associates paid back to the company made it well worth the emotional investment.

## CULTIVATING A FAMILY CULTURE

Would you describe the personal connections among your colleagues as an emotional investment in the success of the company and of each other?

Can you see staying in touch with them years after leaving your current job?

I hope your answers are *Yes.* If not, maybe it's time to consider that you might be the best candidate to change the culture.

The strong sense of community that is a company's glue sticks with people in later years. It's not unlike a fraternity or sorority where the camaraderie continues into later stages of life.

Nostalgia is a wonderful thing. I have found that it can put a smile on your face; it can give you peace of mind in moments when you treasure the gift of fond memories. What you take with you from a work experience inevitably becomes part of your quality of life—hopefully for better, not worse.

I also am grateful to my equity partners for giving me the opportunity to achieve my dreams, at rue21 and afterward, to continue building new business activities. We had a great run together, but it was time for

me to move on to new ventures and start my next chapter. It was the best fifteen-plus years of my career. That's an unusually long time for any CEO and equity group to stay together as a management team with consistent success.

To say that I feel fulfillment from the rue21 family is an understatement. That's not to say I've had enough. It's never enough. Why should it be? I don't call it living to sit back and say, "OK. I'm done." Your life work never is done. It merely has different phases, different *Pieces of the Puzzle*.

Fulfillment isn't final; it should mark a new beginning. Any success you achieve makes you thirst for more. There is no quota on what you can accomplish in a lifetime.

Let's face it. How stimulating is it to sit around and think about what's already been done? Nobody wants to listen to old war stories forever. True stimulation comes from finding more things to do.

For me, the adventure is much more important than the destination. Getting there is satisfying, but before long, I'm itching to take on the next challenge. Moving from one challenge to the next, and then the next, is what builds your career ladder.

# DON'T RETIRE—REVIVE

Don't limit the scope of your career by thinking only in terms of working for a company. I don't work for a company now, and my career is going full steam. You create your own career and how it should be structured. Don't convince yourself that your career should end at some arbitrary point in "retirement." Instead of the word retire, my word is *revive*.

I don't report to a board of directors anymore, but I sit on a board of directors. I no longer sit in a CEO's office, but I advise CEOs. My career has evolved into bolstering other careers. I've gone from building bricks-and-mortar stores to building confidence in **Millennials** and others who value learning from decades of experience and who welcome constructive advice that has been put to the test in real-life situations.

What I set out to do here is use my variety of experiences, lessons learned, accomplishments, and mistakes to help others grow professionally and also become more successful in reaching their personal potential.

Just as satisfying and nostalgic for me as having the largest store count, or going public, or creating a business valued at $1 billion only twelve years after it filed for Chapter 11 bankruptcy, is the human element that lifted rue21 to a rarefied level: *ruebe* achievement awards. *Whatever It Takes* recognition for extraordinary effort. High-energy *"Do you rue?"* videos made by store associates. The *Alter Ego* party. And our best marketing ambassadors—the loyal rue21 customers.

How about you? Apart from relatives, do you enjoy a rapport with people from other generations? Do you try to strike up those relationships or avoid them?

As noted at the beginning of *Fisch Tales*, even when I was a young adult, I related more easily to older adults than did others my age. I respected them, but also was able to see them as people, just like me, whatever their age. As time went on, the same held true in reverse: I felt very comfortable with people who were slightly or even considerably younger than me.

This book is another *Piece of the Puzzle* that I was compelled to create. Once you feel fulfilled in a material way, you still crave emotional fulfillment. One way to achieve that is to ensure the knowledge you have gathered through the years is put to good use, with a shelf life well into the future.

Even when the time arrives that I'm not personally *Mentoring* someone, or being *Mentored* by someone, I want the information and advice I've put out there to continue helping people.

In speaking with *Millennials*, I don't hear that they are fearful of the future as much as I hear that they are not thinking about it too much. That's not good either, of course. I tell them so.

*Not* thinking about it is a form of fearing the future. Face it, embrace it, I tell them. Make your plans for what you want to do with the future, and then figure out the career ladder that will get you there.

You are going to make changes along the way. That's to be expected. I explained in chapter 8 how a new corporate owner of Casual Corner affected my ambitions at that company. Yet, if I hadn't left when I did, the amazing experience I had at rue21 most likely never would have happened.

## YOU *CAN* OFTEN GET WHAT YOU WANT

If anything, I encourage you to accept problems and detours as opportunities to flex your creative problem-solving muscles.

Don't hesitate to **Take a Stand** and **Put It on the Line**! I never regretted doing that. Sometimes you'll get pushback, but so what? You need to learn to deal with that too. Dig in your heels. Make your case. You could be surprised how often you get what you want.

As this book was being written, a discussion arose about whether to use the word "maverick." It's a synonym for **Disruptor**, for not avoiding controversy. I've been described as all the above. It's part of **Putting It on the Line**. Not everybody may be suited to that role, but there are times when you might lose out, or fall behind on your career progress, if you don't insist that what you want is nonnegotiable.

Even if you don't get everything you asked for one time, your tough attitude will be remembered the next time, and people will be careful about how or whether to challenge you. You will have created a reputation as a maverick and as a leader! It's better to regret what you have done than what you haven't done.

Along with your *Career Ladder*, you need to think about your *Vision*. Weird as it sounds for me to say, "Get a *Vision!*" that's exactly what I *am* saying. Your *Vision* keeps you motivated, on track, and hungry to see it come to fruition. Otherwise, you're flying blind.

The *Vision* is your long view. Short term, there's the matter of how others view you, in your workplace and in your industry—I'm talking about your *Persona*. Whether you work for someone or are self-employed, your *Persona* matters. It is how you present yourself. It is how you are perceived. You always must be your authentic self, but sometimes it's necessary to move outside your comfort zone to ensure your *Persona* supports your *Vision*. For example, if your *Vision* is to rise to a leadership position, and you're naturally shy, it may take some work on your part to develop an assertive, take-charge image.

When I was at rue21, "*Do you rue? I do!*" was shorthand for a strong company culture that was all about camaraderie and working closely together in a family atmosphere. It was a rarity among retail chains of our size to enjoy the exciting *esprit de corps* that enlivened our workplace every day. Do I miss that? You bet I do. But the memory of it alone gives me a great sense of fulfillment. Besides, nothing lasts forever. We created it, we sustained it for more than a decade, and we reaped the rewards.

Many people left rue21 feeling enriched in their personal and business lives. That's also a legacy to be proud of, and I am.

## CREATING NEWNESS

If there is a single word that best describes my own *Career Ladder*, it's *newness*. I wasn't interested in simply going with the flow and maintaining the status quo. I had to make my mark wherever I went. The desire to make a difference and raise the stakes for everyone involved burned inside me constantly.

What do I mean by newness? My business model for Casual Corner & Co. kick-started the retail industry's value fashion trend—and rue21 scaled that innovative value specialty store concept into a billion-dollar business.

Newness also is about change. Ironically, some people mistakenly believed that I am a creature of habit who resists change. The record says otherwise.

There's no way I could have built what I did without more than merely embracing change—I initiated change. It doesn't mean I would look to make changes for the sake of change. That's reactive, and my style is to get out in front of trends, not react to them.

I received some criticism because rue21 was not an early adopter of e-commerce. That was by design. Not many retailers were opening more than 100 stores a year during the recession. I didn't want to upset our successful rate of growth by having my team distracted and spread too thin by starting an e-commerce business at that point.

When we decided it was the right time to launch e-commerce sales, that division grew to more than $50 million in sales in a little more than three years.

In the last few years of my tenure at rue21, it had returned to operating as a private company after four years as a high-growth public company. The structure of rue21 changed in succession, from private to public back to private again.

I preferred running the public version of rue21. When it went private again, that was one of the few times in my career that I resisted change, because I didn't agree with the rationale for the changes. I trusted my own instincts more than the data, and probably would do the same again under the same circumstances. Under a different set of circumstances than what occurred, I like to think we could have gone public yet a second time.

Since moving on from rue21 during the 2016 holidays, I've thought a great deal about our slogan, "*Do you rue? I do!*" and what *Meaning* it might have apart from that specific environment and culture that I helped create, and that helped shape who I am now.

*Do you rue?* means finding your groove and enjoying the ride as you figure out where it can take you.

*Do you rue?* means do you embrace life to the fullest?

*Do you rue?* means do you know and care passionately about your purpose?

*Do you rue?* means do you connect constructively with others in a community where you are comfortable?

*Do you rue?* means do you take a stand, have conviction, and *Put It on the Line* to achieve your dreams?

It's always all about people.

*Do you rue?* I (still) do!

# TEN INGREDIENTS OF SUCCESS

These are based on principles mentioned throughout the book that have worked well for me in my career.

**VISION:** The more ambitious, the better. Focus on what you want to achieve now and in the future.

**PEOPLE:** Whether hiring or aligning, value authenticity, dedication, curiosity, and *Tribal Knowledge*. Surround yourself with the best you can find.

**CONNECTING WITH THE CUSTOMER:** Your job is not to indulge yourself or to be defensive. It's to satisfy the customer. You have to think like the customer to win the customer.

**CULTURE:** How a company's attitude and behavior toward associates and customers are codified in its policies and demonstrated in day-to-day business dealings.

**ALIGNMENT:** All team members must be on the same page, pulling in the same direction, carrying their weight.

**TRUST:** Become a student and a judge of human nature. Learn to detect dishonesty and duplicity.

**RISKS:** Playing it safe may keep you securely in place, but also will get you nowhere fast. The road to success is paved with risks worth taking.

**DIVERSIFICATION:** Trends and markets are in constant flux, so reinvention and innovation must be constant.

**SPEED TO MARKET:** A good rule for time management: move toward your goal as quickly as you can without being deterred.

**CONFIDENCE:** Maintaining a strength of focus that refuses to allow the doubts and criticisms of others to weaken your resolve. Don't try to please everybody; just please yourself.

# THE PUZZLE

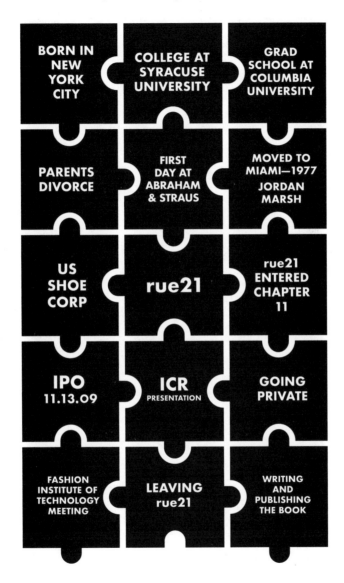

When all the pieces come together, you can see the big picture. Each one of the pieces shaped my journey. But notice that the puzzle is not complete—more pieces can and will fall into place. The same is true for you—whether *Millennial*, *Baby Boomer*, or both, *The Best Is Yet to Come!*

# MILLENNIAL
# ADVISORY BOARD:
# WHO'S WHO

I chose these individuals for their range of expertise and interests to advise me on this book and on future iterations of the *Millennial Baby Boomer* franchise.

From left to right: Brian Tunick, Jeffrey Littman, Bruce Apar, Desiree Nunes, Nicole Manafi Campbell, Robert N. Fisch, Carrie Amber Gaddy, and Rima Reddy

# BRUCE APAR

- **BORN IN:** Astoria (Queens), New York

- **LIVES IN:** Westchester County, New York

- **WRITER, ACTOR, PUN SLINGER, OTHER JOBS AS REQUIRED OR DESIRED**

- **GIGS I HAVE KNOWN:** publisher, editor-in-chief, actor, blogger, fund-raiser, community volunteer

- **HAVE KNOWN BOB SINCE:** high school (it was "Like" at first sight!)

- **WHICH SONG AM I?** "Smile" (by Charlie Chaplin, sung by Nat King Cole)

- **WHAT ABOUT BOB?** After more than a half century of friendship, our relationship never stops growing and deepening. I treasure it more every day. There are times Bob appears to know more about me than I know about myself. Like his daily regimen on the treadmill, Bob's mind runs at full speed 24/7.

- **OTHER KEY INFLUENCERS:** immediate family, Bill O'Brien, Bruce Mishkin

# NICOLE MANAFI CAMPBELL

- **BORN IN:** Berkeley, California

- **LIVES IN:** Williamsburg (Brooklyn), New York

- **GIGS I HAVE KNOWN:** vice president of business development at hedge fund Benefit Street Partners (Franklin Templeton); investment banker at Bank of America Merrill Lynch …

- **… WHICH IS HOW I KNOW BOB.** We worked on the "take private" deal together …

- **… WHICH IS HOW I MET HIM IN 2013.**

- **WHICH SONG AM I?** "Shake It Off" (Taylor Swift)

- **WHAT ABOUT BOB?** Bob lives the principles of laser listening, questioning the status quo, and taking a stand. He shows us that sharing core values can break down perceived barriers of age and status to instead produce deep dialogue and action.

- **OTHER KEY INFLUENCERS:** Mihaly Csikszentmihalyi

# ROBERT N. FISCH

- **BORN IN:** New York City

- **GREW UP IN:** West Hempstead, Long Island, New York

- **LIVES IN:** Miami Heat, N.Y.C. Cool, West Hartford 'burbs

- **GIGS I HAVE KNOWN:** consultant, advisor, mentor, investor, speaker—RNF Group; book author (*Fisch Tales: The Making of a Millennial Baby Boomer);* board of directors—Ollie's; advisory council—Olatec-Biotech; advisor, investor—XRC Lab; founder, president, CEO, and chairman—rue21 ("Do you rue? I still do!"); president—Casual Corner Group

- **WHICH SONG AM I?** "Wake Me Up" (Avicii)

- **KEY INFLUENCERS:** David Simon, Leonardo Del Vecchio, Claudio Del Vecchio, Tom Unrine, Mickey Drexler, Tommy Hilfiger, Stephanie Fisch

# STEPHANIE FISCH

- **BORN IN:** Miami

- **LIVES IN:** Miami, Manhattan, West Hartford (Connecticut)

- **GIGS I HAVE KNOWN:** consultant, beauty and fragrance industry; rue21 fashion and beauty fragrance leadership and marketing

- **HAVE KNOWN BOB SINCE:** 1981

- **WHICH SONG AM I?** "This Is Me" (Keala Settle)

- **WHAT ABOUT BOB?** He has greatly influenced my life because of his passion, his positive attitude, intelligence, and huge heart. He was my mentor before he stole my heart.

- **OTHER KEY INFLUENCERS:** Gabrielle Chanel, Melinda Gates, Freddie Mercury

# CARRIE AMBER GADDY

- **BORN IN:** Charlotte, North Carolina

- **LIVES IN:** Charlotte, North Carolina

- **GIGS I HAVE KNOWN:**
  director, Smile Direct Club; rue21

- **HOW I KNOW BOB:** He was my mentor/CEO at rue21.

- **HAVE KNOWN BOB SINCE:** 2011

- **WHICH SONG AM I?** "This Is Me" (Keala Settle)

- **WHAT ABOUT BOB?** He has challenged me professionally
  and personally to reach far more than I ever imagined I
  could achieve. He is unique and has a greatness in him.
  Bob inspires and pushes everyone around him to share
  in that greatness and challenge the status quo. Bob has
  made the biggest impact on my professional career and
  personal life by teaching me that there are no limits
  to what can be accomplished. I would not be where
  I am today without his mentorship and guidance.

- **OTHER KEY INFLUENCERS:**
  David Katzman, J. K. Rowling

# JEFFREY LITTMAN

- **BORN IN:** Miami

- **LIVES IN:** Arlington, Virginia

- **GIGS I HAVE KNOWN:** financial analyst at a division of Siemens, cryptocurrency researcher; merchant cash advance underwriter

- **HOW I KNOW BOB:** He is my uncle.

- **HAVE KNOWN BOB SINCE:** 1994

- **WHICH SONG AM I?** "Fragments of Time" (Daft Punk)

- **WHAT ABOUT BOB?** His genuine care for others, regardless of their title, makes him special. He creates time for the people who surround him, and he has business sense and experience that can be applied to any situation. I know that when I come to Bob for career advice he will guide me in the right direction.

- **OTHER KEY INFLUENCERS:** Gary Vaynerchuk (a.k.a. Gary Vee)

# DESIREE NUNES (A.K.A. DEZZ)

- **BORN IN:** Houston, but moved to New York when I was three, so I consider myself a full-blown New York girl! Grew up in Pleasantville, New York (Westchester County)

- **LIVES IN:** New York City

- **GIGS I HAVE KNOWN:** private wealth associate at Merrill Lynch, cake pop connoisseur, insurance broker dealer

- **HOW I KNOW BOB:** He is my executive advisor on FOMO (fear of missing out) and JOMO (joy of missing out)

- **HAVE KNOWN BOB SINCE:** 2017 (but it seems like a lifetime)

- **WHICH SONG AM I?** "Paradise" (Coldplay)

- **WHAT ABOUT BOB?** He constantly encourages me to step outside my comfort zone and think big, while always reassuring me that "the best is yet to come." We share thoughts with each other, and I always leave our conversations feeling inspired and thinking with a different perspective.

- **OTHER KEY INFLUENCERS:** Diane Von Furstenberg, Derek Jeter

# RIMA REDDY

- **HOMETOWN:** Pittsburgh, Pennsylvania; Scottsdale, Arizona

- **LIVES IN:** New York City

- **GIGS I HAVE KNOWN:** principal, XRC Labs (Consumer/ Retail Accelerator/VC), Goldman Sachs, Ralph Lauren

- **HOW I KNOW BOB:** Through XRC Labs

- **HAVE KNOWN BOB SINCE:** 2017

- **WHICH SONG AM I?** "Let's Go" (Calvin Harris and Ne-Yo)

- **WHAT ABOUT BOB?** He understands people's personalities and their thoughts in a way that I've rarely seen in other people I've met. He has helped me think seriously about what's right for me to do as I move ahead in my career—and in my life.

- **OTHER KEY INFLUENCERS:** Kirsten Green, Marty Chavez

# BRIAN TUNICK

- **HOMETOWN:** Woodmere, New York

- **LIVES IN:** Manhattan

- **GIGS I HAVE KNOWN:** sell-side research analyst for retail sector at Royal Bank of Canada and at Bear Stearns/ J. P. Morgan; angel investor; professional BBQ eater

- **HAVE KNOWN BOB SINCE:** rue21 initial public offering on Nov. 13, 2009

- **WHICH SONG AM I?**
  "If Today Was Your Last Day" (Nickelback)

- **WHAT ABOUT BOB?** Ever since we worked together on the rue21 initial public offering, I knew Bob looked at the world differently. He trusted himself enough to run his company by his own rules, even when it would have been safer to follow the consensus. Seeing how strong the results were while he ran the company, he clearly was right to trust his own gut.

- **OTHER KEY INFLUENCERS:**
  John McEnroe, Jeff Bezos, Ralph Lauren, Jamie Dimon